OGOEGO by Ricky Garni

Begun in January 2016 and finished in December 2106

KIASSIK SAN NO 3 URWT 9 pt font employed

Cover Design and Photograph by the author, NYC: 2015

ISBN # 978-1-365-89686-6

® 2017 courtesy of 101 Secret Wing Dings (FEH 5313)

OTHER WORKS BY THE AUTHOR

Peppermint (1995)

Soft White (1995)

Michelle (1996)

Photos & Abstracts (1996)

Much Business (1997)

Lözé (1997)

Gall (1998)

Xipo (1998)

Fred (1998)

Bill (1998)

Wilma (1998)

Cloud Writing (1998)

A Perfect Day (1998)

Hombre (1999)

Wardrobe (1999)

The Pillow Enigmas (1999)

Vermilion & Golden Light (2000)

Intimate Portraits (2000)

Holidays (2000)

Apartment Stories, I & II (2000)

New Mushrooms (2001)

Missing (2001)

Pommes Frites (2002)

Age of Anxiety (2003)

27 Round Sounds (2003)

October (2004)

Make It Wavy (2006)

Make It Too Wavy (2007)

Comments without Cosmos (2008)

My Favorite Fifteen Presidents (2008)

Make It Long & Wavy (2008)

Christine (2008)

Maybe Wavy (2009)

Eternal Journals of Crispy Flotilla (2010)

2% Butterscotch (2011)

Dots (2012)

HEY (2013)

The Sea of Kicking Legs (2014)

Wander (2014)

Jiggle Fest (2015)

The We Book (2015)

The Pinky Embrace (2015)

X-Y (2015)

Divisive Potatoes (2016)

"Something feels like it's missing when I haven't heard any music, and when I hear music, then I really feel like something is missing. That's the best I can do in trying to describe music."

– Robert Walser, A Schoolboy's Diary and Other Stories

"So you, too, like fruitcake?"
(on meeting Lenin in Zurich during World War I.)

– Robert Walser

OGOEGO

2017

INSIDE AND OUT

Isn't it strange that you can sit down in a restaurant
and order flowers because you don't feel good because
you are hungry. And then you eat the flowers and you feel
much better, while outside the restaurant flowers are feeling
very bad, because of thirst they are dying.

LITTLE DOT IN DOTLAND

I don't remember what she did for a living or how she spent her time or her deepest fears or darkest secrets. I just remember that everywhere she went, there were a lot of dots. And everywhere she didn't go, there were no dots.

THE SANITARY FISH MARKET

A little mountain of cabbage slightly pickled.
It's smaller than a mountain. It's smaller than
a hill. It's a little hill. It sits on top of a crab cake.
The crab feels cool and calm because the cabbage
is cool and calm.

A LITTLE BROWN DOG FROM A COUNTRY & WESTERN SONG

A little brown dog with bright blue eyes was locked inside
a banana-yellow car. The little dog yelped until someone
approached the car, and then he trembled and pressed
his nose near the little crack of the window.
This is a day that the little dog will remember for the rest
of his life. He will try to forget it, though, as best he can,
by playing with his squeezee-toy and chewing on a
preposterously large hunk of rawhide in the backyard
and running and barking loudly at the mail truck every
afternoon until he is too old to run and bark at
the mail truck anymore.

THE WORLD'S FAIR

I have three real friends and two animatronic friends. My real friends won't last forever, but my animatronic friends will. They even told me that they will help me bury my real friends. But they also told my real friends they will help to bury me.

PIZZA TIME

My son asked me if I would like a church funeral.
He asked when we were ordering pizza from
the pizza truck. I think because it took so long
to make, but when it came out, it was delicious –
the crust with thick and flaky, and there was
a single basil leaf on each of the slices
(although there were only four of them.)
Still, they ran out of boxes, and so we had to
carry it home, wrapped in tin foil, and quickly,
before they were too cold to eat.

I DON'T WANT TO SAY GOODBYE
The Worst Movie I Ever Saw

A cow in a field and a man and a gun.

ICE DRUMMING HAS A SURPRISINGLY UNIQUE AND PLEASANT SOUND

Many Russian Ladies jumped upon the ice of Lake Baikal
and the sounds of the ladies against the ice was so
beautiful

that ever since that day their husbands have come out
to the ice of Lake Baikal and performed beautiful and
elaborate drum patterns

using their fingers on the ice much to the pleasure
of ice fishers and farmers and children and furry dogs
who live in the small houses that line Lake Baikal

during the long and beautiful winters in this foreboding
universe filled with ice upon a planet that looks like ours

that contains a Russia and a Lake Baikal also a billion miles
away from anything we know other than these few and
beautiful things: ice, fishing, dogs, husbands, wives, Russia.

AJAX

Your entire life is real except for candied apples.
You dreamt candied apples and never knew it.
So go back and think about your life, and just
remove any parts that ever mentioned candied
apples. That is the life you have had so far.

Now someday you might even come upon candied apples.
But you won't even be expecting it. You will be surprised.
You will be excited. You will think you are dreaming but

You are not. But then again, they might not be real
candied apples.

MY CAR

has a large key. The top of the key is covered in rubber.
The rubber is black. Right now I am thinking: when was
the last time I saw something in rubber that wasn't black?
And also: is rubber black when it comes from a rubber tree?
Rubber trees are in Thailand.

What They Say

They say car was "Made in the USA" but the rubber from
my car key was made in Thailand and here's what you do:
You bleed rubber trees of their rubber (which is sticky and
milky and gooey) and then you make rubber things from
them. You have to do a lot to the rubber first.

Uncured Rubber

"Uncured rubber has relatively few uses." Cured rubber, many.
Just look at your shoes! (The bottoms of them.) There's rubber
and chewing gum. Cured rubber is called "Vulcanized Rubber"
and who doesn't like the word "Vulcanized"?

Rubber Nostalgia

When I was little, I tried to make up new expressions because
I was tired of words like "Groovy." I tried "Vulcanized!" but no one in my class
ever used it, or at least like I did. Some spoke of their vulcanized sneakers.
Most of the people I know are inclined towards rubber, but that is a good thing.

Acceptance

Once, long ago, they said, "You will make a great doctor."
But I didn't. There was a movie called RUBBER. No one saw it.
This is the problem with rubber. My car was named after
a planet, but I don't like it. Don't like planets either. I like rubber.

I like the feel of it and the feel of the word when I use a pen to write it. Goddam, but I really do.

POEM IN FIVE PARTS

Wednesday

The golden flowers reach towards the window and out towards the cherry tree. The red flowers sit below the awning and rest.

The Happiest People in the Whole World

Own one guitar their whole lives. When
their house burns down, they rush in to find it.

Grammar And Loss

Once a man had a horse. Now a horse simply is.

Cigarettes Are Bad For You

Unless you dance.

I Wish

I had slept next to you since the day I was born.

THE CHOPIN FROWN

There is only one photograph in existence of Chopin,
and in it he is not smiling. I don't think you were supposed to smile
in photographs in the 19th century. But wouldn't it be nice if you had
only one photograph of yourself, and in that photograph, you were smiling?
Chopin probably never thought about that. Nor did he ever look
at the photograph and say to himself: this is this and that is that and
I am not smiling about it.

SNOW GLOBE

In the south, we put the snow globes in the freezer, so that when we took them out and smashed them with a hammer, the snow would be cold. Sometimes there would be little yellow ducks that would be struggling inside to escape the cold. They would float down the river. We try to scoop them up before they could find another globe.

INVENTORY

In my hands is a flip book with everything I ever owned.
If you flip the cards really fast, it looks just like a movie.
The last frame is a flip book and on the back of the book
is a garbage can.

POUGHKEEPSIE

Because of the hand grenade's natural tendency
to resemble a pineapple

It is not unusual for a soldier's mouth to water
when he is about to lob a hand grenade

Much as it is natural for a child to cover his ears when
he sits down for a delicious dinner on a faraway island

Or at a restaurant that says
"We serve hand grenades" – in Poughkeepsie.

Yet you must feed the soldier
and you must not scold the child

Nor should you praise the child
for the child was quite rude
But why?

What was the child thinking?
Whatever it was, he must stop

Stop child, stop

Do not think those thoughts
of paradise

4

What do you think about? I think about standing in the middle of the road
and watching the sun rise out of the ocean. It is windy and warm.
I am four years old. I am saying: "It's great to be young."

But why should I be saying that then? I don't.
I watch the sun rises until it is a complete circle.

WOODSTOCK

What I can't understand is that her clear, naked body
is covered in rain, and there is rain all around her,
but everything else is so blurry because of the rain
that you can't see anything or anyone except her,
and she is smiling and clapping, and you can see
that so well, and you can see her brown hair,
and nothing else can you see.

THE DIFFERENT PARTS OF THE ORCHESTRA, PT. I

The bassoon is almost as red as it is brown.
It is a complicated color that was invented
by the orchestra way back when.

It lives life richly. It can be a dying bear
when it sings, a smiling hippo when it is
at rest. It is not the same. It is different.

Anything that is different is easy
to make fun of. Go on, make fun
of it. Make fun of the bassoon. Just remember:
someday, you might need the bassoon.

KLAUS

Marin made Klaus Nomi into a felt doll. Klaus Nomi sang
like an opera singer behind famous rock stars. Nobody knew
who Klaus Nomi really was or where he came from. Some
said Germany, some said Jupiter. Some said: Mars.

Klaus Nomi's body was made of triangles. He was black
and white and had a tuxedo and his little lips were bright red.
When he sang your body would break out in gooseberries.

When Klaus Nomi died, some said he went to *this* planet, others said no,
he went to *that* planet. Klaus Nomi became ordinary for just a second, went
to some place, and then back again. And then he left once more, and went to
heaven somewhere. When I stop and listen in the dark, I hear his red lips.

SEQUENCE

Why is a 100 lb sack of potatoes so much more difficult
to carry to bed than you? I will never know unless you
let me carry you to bed, which you should, because you
are tired and pale. It has been a long day, and I have carried
many potatoes this day, and today, you are unwell.
Come – let me take you to bed, let me make you
a nice bowl of *vichyssoise,* let me love you, let me do
what I can do, it's all that I can do.

DENTAL FLOSS

is amazing and satisfying and thin and stretchy and long
and makes a sound when you pull it out and wrap it tightly
around your fingers and it snaps off neatly around your fingers
and turns your fingers nova-white and is quite cheap you don't
have to be a millionaire to buy it and it lasts forever and I guess
you could make a guitar strings out of it if you want to and you
could take guitar lessons and play the guitar with its strings and
people would say "that's beautiful!" and you would become famous
and perhaps even a millionaire and you would smile and smile.

HARD KNOCKING

Just think: the woman who you might love you just passed by.
She was sipping tea in a coffee shop, and you passed by
because you do not drink coffee. But you drink tea.
But you lack courage to enter a coffee house and
order tea. She did not. But you like tea. But not coffee.
Or coffee houses. But she does. And so you passed coffee by.
And so you passed tea by. And so you passed her by

on your bicycle which is beautiful and
rare and so fast in the wind!

WHEN

When they painted the wrinkles on the fur coat
on the Eskimo Boy holding a double dip ice cream
cone on top of the Dairy Queen they must have done
it on a beautiful day with crystal blues skies because
the wrinkles are the color of a beautiful blue sky unless
they did it indoors and they recalled the precise shade
of the blue of a beautiful sky as Hannibal Lecter once did,
drawing the Duomo as seen from the Belvedere.

PRESCRIPTIONS

Going to a new grocery makes you feel like the world
is a wonderful place. Going to a grocery store at 7
in the morning to buy milk makes you feel like the world
is a wonderful place. Going to the grocery store late at night
and no one is there at all makes you feel like the world is
a wonderful place. Let's face it: going to a grocery store
in general makes you feel like the world is a wonderful place –
a wonderful place chock full of grocery stores. The parking is
often awful just impossible, ridiculous and yet, it is a wonderful place.

WHAT HAPPENS WHEN YOU DIE

You keep going, only everything works that didn't work before.
For example: that taxi is now free, the wind is there, soft on your neck,
and the little sparrow, fallen from a tree, confused and frightened in the street,
is now resting comfortably in that very tree in which it longed to be.

DOUBLE BLIND

If I were blind, I could not tell you how beautiful
those starlings are in the sky. If we were both blind,
I could. And you could say *yes, so beautiful.*

MATH PROBLEM

There is such a difference between going to the grocery store
at dawn to get biscuits and coming home and someone is still asleep
upstairs and going to the grocery store at dawn to get biscuits and
coming home.

OBIT

She had Mona Lisa's neck and now the only one left with Mona Lisa's neck is Mona Lisa.

1961

In the photograph, I am pointing at something just to the left
of the photographer. Whatever it was, is gone now. It either died
or moved or changed into something completely different.
If I were to go back to that exact spot (and I know where it is,
right near the mango tree in the backyard) – and if were I to point
in the same direction, what would I be pointing at?

Something that will die or move, or change into something else.
Perhaps it will change into what it was when I pointed at it the first time.
Perhaps it was someone I loved, who loved standing under the mango tree.

COMMUNIQUÉ

Let's say you want to write a letter to a mountain lion.
You have a piece of paper, an envelope, and a pen.
You write the letter and you seal it in the envelope.
What do you do then? You go to the post office
and buy a stamp.

TESTAMENT

When I am a skeleton in a box being pushed into a wall of fire, I am going to do a lot of writing about it on asbestos looseleaf with a steel pencil and a small eraser I can fit in my nightgown.

DELICIOSO!

By the time I pronounce *bruschetta* correctly
as many times as I pronounced *bruschetta*
incorrectly, I will be an old man, and no longer
able to afford *bruschetta,* and if I can afford
bruschetta, I will no longer know what it is
and I will ask "What's that?" and they will say
"bruschetta" and I will say, "Who cares, Tommy?
I for one, do not." And then I will eat *bruschetta*
and I will enjoy it, and they will say: "Tony."

APRÈS MOVIE

The strangest thing happened last night. I fell asleep
in the movie theatre and woke up during the dream sequence.
When I asked a stranger about the dream sequence, he said
there wasn't a dream sequence, and tipped his hat to me as he left.

I think he wore a beautiful black hat.

That exploded.

HEADS UP

Ann Hodges was the only person in the world who was ever hit by a meteor.

It left a bruise that looked like a black jellyfish. When I was little I threw rocks at them so they would pop. Meteors would fall from the sky but I was so fast that they missed me and hit my friend Anne, who claimed to be innocent.

CLASS NOTES

Two things that I have never seen
in the same room together
are a madman and
a straw hat.

MUSIC THEORY

You don't have to be a captain
of jazz to sail the high seas at dawn

All you need is a crayon
and a piece of paper onto

Which can be drawn
a golden saxophone

POST CAR

After the car crash, each of them walked away from the car, fanning further and further into the field, with their hands together as though holding musical instruments. In a way, they all wrote a song together that night, which some say was quite beautiful, while others said it wasn't beautiful at all, and the rest said it seemed somewhat beautiful, but strange, and yet, sweetly familiar.

THE HINDENBURG & THE TITANIC

One was afraid of water, and one was afraid of air.
They were both grey.

PLAYBOY BUNNIES: DECEMBER 1953 to DECEMBER 1954

December 1953: a soft red curtain

January 1954: a crushed blue/aquamarine
curtain and a red shag carpet

February 1954: a clamshell mirror, pearls,
a shoulder belt of red sequin stars

March 1954: a blue ribbon, a jet-silver cushion
with pink trim and white tassels

April 1954: blue velvet carpet, shaped
like a mountain and red roses

May 1954: a very large zebra's skin (huge)

June 1954: a pale yellow telephone
and black opera gloves

July 1954: a dead tiger with claws and red trim

August 1954: topographical red rug
with yellow sparkles

September 1954: a white candle and
a white bow and a red seat cover

October 1954: a footstool covered
in more silver crushed fabric

November 1954: a straw hat and
November-yellow beach chair

December 1954: a transparent nightgown
and barbed wire

SECRET SERVICE

We are so used to watching them on television or in the movies. But every time that the camera focuses on the agents, the music commences: a dull, droning sound in the background, getting louder and louder, measure by measure. *Someone is going to try to shoot the President!*

If you are a real secret service agent, you hear that droning all the time, from the time you adjust your crisp white shirt in the morning until you remove your wrinkly white shirt in the evening. But you never hear the sound of the gun, only that droning sound. Imagine in the morning, eating a bowl of Rice Krispies, and there it is again, that terrible, awful sound.

BEHEST

I want to have a daughter so that we can go to the bakery together on a sunny Saturday morning and when she asks What is that Daddy I can say with confidence: That my dear, my angel, my love, my sweet is a

brioche.

POOF

She put all of her thoughts into a ship.
And turned the ship around.
And headed towards the shore.

COMPANY

Walking upstairs, I imagine I hear someone.
But it is no one, instead, who is making a sound.

DREAM NAPPING

When I was a little boy I wanted to be a lawyer.
Now I want to be an astronaut flying through
the galaxies, looking for lawyers to fly through
the galaxies with.

DEMI MOORE RELEASES STATEMENT
AFTER MAN FOUND DEAD IN HER POOL

"There was a man in my pool. He was dead. It's really strange to think there's a dead man in your pool. Normally you say, 'There's someone in my pool. He's splashing and having a gay old time.' But I can't say this today. I can only say there's a man in my pool. He's not having a gay old time. Nor does he appear to be splashing, nor will he soon, or even later, appear to splash."

UNREQUITED LOVE

Sometimes I tell people from the north what pretend snow is like, and they tell me what real snow is like, and we both can hardly believe each other, and sometimes we say "I hope to see this other snow of which you speak and which you speak of so fondly – someday."

.

THINGS I LEARNED FROM THE ZAPPA FAMILY

There is a street in Sicily named Zammata which means:
The Sound of Children's Feet, Playing in the Rain.

SCHEDULES

For years I looked at your photograph before I went to bed.
And then I began to look at the fireplace, instead, and my
favorite spot there, where the smoke rises from a space
between the logs and curls up around the top log like
a thin grey blanket. Above the fireplace is a photograph
of you. But lately I have considered moving it across
the room, so that it would face the fireplace,
while I sit by the fireplace, looking across the room
for you.

GLASS HALF FULL

They found a million year old dog with his brains still intact. But the dog was smart enough to realize that none of that mattered anymore. It would be nice to lie out in the sun now, the dog thought to himself, and just feel the breeze.

A SLINKY HAS NO CHOICE

But to go downstairs. Downstairs has the living room,
the rec room, and the kitchen.

It also has a view of the harbor and in the morning,
the light sparkles on the water.

But upstairs has the bedroom, and a view of the mountain.
It cannot use its springy torso

to go upstairs, because a springy torso cannot do that.
Still, if "a Slinky has no choice but to go downstairs"

then the Slinky must have been upstairs, once.
Perhaps his wife carried him upstairs.
Perhaps she could do it again –

as long as she realizes the bedroom is where her Slinky
wants to go. As long as she has the strength. As long as
his wife is

not a Slinky, too.

PASTORAL for HAROLD LLOYD

A beautiful little cottage with a thatched roof
and a big chimney and a little girl at the doorway
with her father holding her and waving "Hello! Goodbye!"
because they both hello and goodbye apply as they see
each other in the distance and as they wander back inside
the cottage where it is warm and friendly and they are happy
in this home this place and

where from this place many years later the father
will go away and then many years later the little girl
will go away and then years later the cottage, too,
will go away and do its best
 to find them.

OPERATOR

If you stand side by side with someone you can put your arm
around their waist and stare out the window and say I love you
and they won't hear it

as long as it is a busy restaurant with waiters who clumsily
drop things like glasses and trays

and so you are safe as long as you don't want them to hear it
but do you want them to hear it

you better decide to be loud because I see a waiter coming
and he is carrying a humongous tray of Chicken Alfredo
and he is looking out the window and he has a mustache
and he is not steady on his small fine feet

23 & ME

This one banyan tree is the first tree I ever saw.
And so I go back to this one banyan tree whenever
I can and ask "How are you doing?" and if it doesn't
say anything I will say "You probably don't remember me"
which is probably true but then it's been so long that this
might not be the same banyan tree. It might just be
his little boy.

CLOSE CAPTIONED AL FRESCO

I saw a movie that was filmed in France.
The wind blew through the forest,
saying woosh woooosh woosh wooooo
and there were subtitles. They read:

Woosh Wooooosh Woosh Woooooo

THE TORSO OF ROBERT MITCHUM

Robert Mitchum's torso was shaped like a top.
And when he was young, it was easy to explain
what his torso looked like if someone asked you.
"It looks like a top." When he was young, everyone
played with tops. Even little boys with small chests.

But by the time Robert Mitchum died, nobody played
with tops. But people no longer asked about his
chest. They would ask questions like: "How did
Robert Mitchum die?" Which is harder to answer.
Everyone dies in their own peculiar way.

WISHING WELL

When I fall in love I want to run through the forest
and chase deer, for the deer are always in the forest,
waiting for me, because when they fall in love they can't
wait to see me so that they can run away.

When neither of us are in love, we just stay where
we are and wait.

Sometimes I am in the forest with the deer. Sometimes
I am in another forest without the deer. Sometimes I like
to draw a picture of a deer, looking for a forest, or me.

GET DOWN, MOSEY

The definition of mosey
"walk or move in a leisurely manner"
makes me relax when I read it.

Whenever I need to relax, I read
the word 'mosey.' If I can't find it,
I say it. If I can't say it, I mosey
about to get in the mood to find it.

VAUDEVILLE

premature babies in bottles
rats in jockey silks,
riding cats

STATUE OF LIBERTY

If you were a sculptor, what would happen
if you made a twenty foot face?

You would be so tired. And every night
as you went to bed
you would think to yourself:

neck, torso, genitals, thighs, knees, toes...

CHARACTER STUDY

The squirrel outside my house stands at attention
when I jiggle my keys.

When I throw peanuts and pecans on the sidewalk,
he runs away.

Here's what I conclude: though not hungry,
the squirrel longs for adventure.

Perhaps if he could drive my car
that would be an adventure.

Or let's say *a* car. The brakes on my car don't work:
now *that* would be an adventure.

But this is not an the sort of adventure a normal squirrel
would desire.

But I am not a normal squirrel.

DOUBLE A LAMB

My toy lamb sounds like the ocean if you depress the button on his spine that is marked "Ocean" underneath the button that is marked "Baaah."

LOVE LETTER

When the Pancake House closed, a thousand waffles cheered. But here's the funny part: they – pancakes, waffles – are exactly the same thing. Usually.
But these are quite different – those, there. We like this about them and we love pancakes. Waffles are the same, though, and we hate them for it.

SIX SHOOTER

My favorite toy was a gun shaped like a finger only the fingernail
was painted flesh color which is what I loved best about it except
that it fired darts and little caps that make a tiny bit of smoke when
you shot it, but it could not kill anybody and it made it almost impossible
to play *Tarantella* on the piano which I hated anyway but I played it in
a recital because it was so elegant and mysterious, probably still is
if you were to hear it today.

DEEP FREEZE

Tonight there will be a deep freeze.
Take care to cover your hydrangeas.
There also will be snow in Pennsylvania.
And dancing bears in Alaska.

This afternoon I will be busy buying hydrangeas.
Because I like to cover things and live a life of secrecy.
I mean, they do. Until it's warm.
And then they don't.

When I buy goats, which I do
I feed them to the doctors
because of what the doctors do
to the goats. It's a long story

From a movie I saw which was quite good:
let me tell you all about it.

An entrepreneur, his unraveling.
His wife who loved him living
in their crumbling mansion.

His son who shot himself in the living room.
The people who believed and then didn't.

After the movie, we had a hamburger.
And listened to quiet Beethoven.
It wasn't frozen yet.

We quietly pulled up to where we were
and before you went away
you shined the light on my door
so I could see where to put the key

And so I put the key there
and then I said I think I'll stay here
and then I did I stayed there
I stayed there forever
and then I left

AN ESSAY ON SCISSORS

I love scissors. What they can do is amazing. In fact everything they can do is amazing. If it wasn't, there would be the opposite of scissors somewhere but there is not. And there would be people who would say "Scissor are terrible!" but again, there are not. With scissors, you can take things that were once here, and put them there, in smaller little shapes, or even in small bits, if you are really excited and love doing it. You can change things so that you don't even know what they are anymore. You can hold them up and say "See here"
to somebody. You can paint them a nice red color.

I have done a million things with scissors, and I still find new things to do with scissors every day. Today, for example,
I am going to cut the sun out of the sky with my scissors.
And then the moon and the cow and all of the grass.
And then the house and the children playing in the yard.
And then I will rest. And then I will go on a date.
I will probably even get kissed but if I don't,
the good thing is, I have, at home, scissors.
Many, in fact. Late at night, if I don't get kissed,
and it hasn't been such a good night, I will be
surrounded by scissors.

MARRIAGE

I took a photograph of a beautiful painting in the museum and just as I did a girl walked in front of the painting. I took the photograph because I liked the painting; now I like the girl. Someday, she will slowly turn around. Who will she be then? She will be a painting then. She will remind me of when I loved painting more than anything.

VISIONARIES

Lenses are included with purchase, so there is glass between the world and everything you see. In a way, you are always safe indoors.

MUSIC IS A HILL OF BEANS

War is terrible.
The celesta is good.
Conductors are brave.
Symphonies are songs
that lose their minds

CONDUCT

When the violinist enters the stage,
everyone in the audience trusts that
he actually can play the violin.
The other musicians trust that he can
play the violin. The conductor trusts that
he can play the violin. The violinist isn't
sure if he can play the violin, but he thinks
that it would be fun to try now that everyone
is so quiet. And then

somebody coughs.

RAINCOAT

The oilskin was once made of sailcloth
and a thin layer of tar.

Then canvas duck and linseed oil.
The words of another century are

so beautiful as they take you
by the arm and say

let's get out of the rain
or
out of this train

CARROT

When she died I stared for hours at a photo of her in
a carrot-colored sweater. Sometimes I wish she had
just become a carrot like her sweater instead.
Then I could have planted her in a little planter
on the window sill and soon I would see all sorts
of carrots growing – a little bit of orange and a lot
of green and then – what's this? A little orange again?
And is that a little bit of green? Well, then –
off I must go to get a bucket of water.

Every day I see the sun kiss carrots in the morning. Every night
I see the moon make them soft and warm. Beneath the soil
these carrots grow bigger and bigger, and there are more
and more carrots, and they are much too beautiful to eat,
and I just don't know what to do, and I am almost at the end
of my rope, until one day she knocks on the door, in her
carrot-colored sweater, saying It's me It's me and Oh good!
I think to myself and then I say Oh no, oh no. I think both. I do.
And I drop my bucket. I do not mean to.

SAM'S REAL NAME IS GRAHAM

Sam gave me a blueberry swirl ice cream cone
with a dollop of chiffon on top. What's this?
I asked him. The earth, Sam said.

In outer space it is so cold
that ice cream never melts.

CARTOONS

When someone received a knock on the head
with a hammer or an anvil a huge banana would
grow out of their scalp.

For years I couldn't eat bananas and I was worried
when I saw a hammer. I never saw an anvil. Now
I realize that I actually

like bananas. I just don't like head bananas.
Sometimes I look for an anvil, but not very
enthusiastically. When I really need one, it will

show up. In the meantime, I shall move to a country
of bananas and I shall be pleased with the things
I find there; of course the danger of the unknown
will also excite me.

3 WORDS THAT HUMPHREY BOGART PRONOUNCES STRANGELY

Maraschino Cherry

Coupé

Tomato

2/3 of them are food words

1/3 of them we don't say anymore

1/3 of them we don't eat because they are too sweet

FRITES

We like pretending this restaurant is a good restaurant when
it is actually a bad restaurant. "How is your steak frites?" I ask. "Delicioso!"
She replies. "Care for a tasty Prosecco?" "I most certainly would" she replies.

What would happen if this bad restaurant was a good restaurant? It would
be really hard to act as though it was a bad restaurant, because we would
be enjoying it too much and it would show in our faces. Besides, it's not
nice to be mean.

Our waiter pretends he is taking our order.
But really, he is a small white dove
circling the peaks
of Karl's Church
in Vienna
at dawn.

CONVERSATION ABOUT LOOPY BELTS: 1969

I don't want one of those loopy belts.
You should get one of those loopy belts.

Uncertain if the conversation occurred in that order.
It is more likely that it occurred in the following order:

You should get one of those loopy belts.
I don't want one of those loopy belts.

The conversation concluded at that point
and there was a trip to the shopping mall
that followed.

The conversation concluded at that point
and there was no trip to the shopping mall
that followed.

BLUE AND ORANGE BOXES

Every time I bought rock candy, it was four o'clock in the afternoon, and the sky was dark, and it was about to rain.

FIRST YOU MUST LOVE YOURSELF

In my dream, toilet paper was called vanity paper.

AT THE PETSHOP

You know, that little pig
will not always be so tiny.

AT THE TOYSTORE

That's a nice little pig.

AT TWO

I am listening to an interview
of Audrey Hepburn from 1959.
She is speaking French and stirring tea.
She stirs it constantly because she is nervous.
She speaks in French and her voice is beautiful.
She often says the word "ballet" — in French.

In 1992 Audrey Hepburn is giving an interview
in French. She is not stirring tea she is only talking.
Her voice is not as beautiful but she is quite beautiful.
There are no French police cars passing by the window.

Like the French police cars that were passing
by the window in 1959.
When I listened to that interview
with Audrey Hepburn, in French.

Did I say "listen"?
I was watching that interview in French.
I am watching this interview in French.
Although you don't really watch anything
in French. You just watch.

Now she is saying "Gigi."
And one more time, "Ballet."
And I am drinking tea, too.

TRAVEL

Is it true that when someone shoots you,
you can see the bullet coming towards you,
and the bullet looks like a little clock,
and at the moment that it arrives you can hear
the alarm go off and you wake up in or of heaven
and say *Good Morning to you* and yawn?

RAPSCALLIONS

They are feeding LSD to the bison of Montana.
This is not good. The bison are interested in LSD
but it is not good for them at all. The owners
of the bison are understandably furious about this.
Bison cannot do the things that bison should do –
like romp and mount – when they are
hallucinating. What can they do about these
acid-snacking bison? What will transpire with the bison
population if the culprits do not desist?
What will the world feel like when you can
no longer say "Out there in the prairie –
I think I spotted some bison" when the fields
seem to glow
in the pale light
of their limitless beauty?

It is worth keeping in mind that the bison eat the LSD
the first time out of politeness. The second time,
out of desire.

LIFE STORY

The rain was so powerful that it nearly
blew off the door in at the movie theatre
while in the movie Hitler surveyed
the Louvre and said: "Yes, that's exactly
the way it should look."

Meanwhile I am in my dungarees
and I am looking for my yo yo.

Have you seen my yo yo?

I lost it here as a child.

RADIOHEAD

If your pool is the shape of a moon, and the sky is clear and the moon is out and full and in just the right place you will have a moon in your backyard that you can jump into. A few minutes later, the devil will have taken the moon away, and your moon place will be filled with stars, just ripe for into-jumping.

SHE WOULDN'T SAY SHE WAS OUTSIDE A WINDOW

A little girl is playing outside the window with her fluffy
orange dog. The orange is sort of the color of Orange
Julius, but I don't think that they make Orange Julius
anymore. I think the company went out of business.
Once upon a time you saw them everywhere,
in the shopping malls and on the streets ,
and they were frothy and delicious.

Now the fluffy orange dog has run away.
The little girl gives chase.

1833

The best part of the ox for roast is the thick part of the thin flank.

SEARS & ROEBUCK

The families in clothing ads don't really know each other.
I am not sure why I didn't realize this before.

THE REVISOR

If you ice skate backwards on Michigan Avenue in Chicago —
Wait. There is no good way to end this sentence.

Let's try again.

If you are skating backwards on Lake Michigan
on a beautiful, frosty day...

LET'S GO TO CHARLOTTESVILLE

Everyone who wants to go to Charlottesville says that.
Even the people who live in Miami and Crystal River.

And they have porpoises and sea cows and grass.
But Charlottesville has all those things.

They have pictures of them in their very great university.
It was founded by Thomas Jefferson who once said:

"If everybody is smart, then everybody is smart"
although some people disagree with that.
They say: "...then everybody is dummkopf."

But *they* are dummkopfs. Also in Charlottesville.
You will find many brick buildings and pianos.
And vinegar and hills. Once I saw a man with a limp.

There are cool rivers that refresh you.
As they once did the Founding Fathers.
Who had no desire to go to Florida.

Let's go to Charlottesville! They said.
They wore white hats and breeches.
They felt the breeze within their breeches.

And were ready to go.
But there they
already were.

INVENTORY

A giant rotating cylinder of chocolate marbled white and milk.

A man grates the chocolate as it rotates and places the grated chocolate in a crepe filled with nutella and dark chocolate syrup.

I take a nap and dream about chocolate. All sorts of chocolate.

When I awake, I look for the film again. It's gone.

In its place is a movie about a two legged goat.

The goat is in a tree chewing green leaves.

He is so happy in his tree.

I want a crepe.

I want a tree.

I want that damn goat.

REGIMEN

He waved at me from his exercycle like he knew me
and I waved back from my exercycle like I knew him
but I didn't know him and he didn't know me however
his father knew my father and his father invented
the exercycle and my father rode the exercycle and
then his father had kids and my father had kids and
we all rode exercycles and then his father had
a heart attack and died but people don't blame
the exercycle for his father dying they blame
his kids who were just rotten it was their fault
and my father was just fine and didn't die and
we loved each other for a long time and
he always said "You kids are great!" and
we always said "We love you, Dad!" and
then of course he died eventually but not
from us but from the cancer or maybe from
the drink.

SERMON

Running must be fun and
scary if you are blind.

TROPHY

I have learned how to take pills super well.
I wish someone would buy me an ice cream cone.
Like my mother did when I learned how to roller skate.
Such a good boy!

PROBABILITY

When you are in a swing
and you are going up so high in the air
that you think you will leave the seat
and go all the way around the world

you are both afraid and excited all at once
even though you know this has only happened
one other time ever and this was when the idea

of a swing set in space was relatively new
and it transpired on a bright day in May
and it happened a long time ago

and it wasn't me or you who thought of it
it was a man in a purple hat

PLAYING THE PIANO IN A SPORTING HOUSE

I became distracted by Jelly Roll Quilt.
And then Jelly Roll Song.
And then, Jelly Roll Race —
until I discovered that was
a race for Jelly Roll Quilts.

Anyway, his real name was Ferdinand.
But he preferred:
Mr. Jelly Roll.

Stabbed

In the chest and face.
But he didn't die
He died later.
Before that,
he married Mabel,
a showgirl.

Bumptious

None of his admirers attended his funeral.
His personality was too bumptious.
But Duke Ellington — you heard of him?
He wasn't there, either.

Not Icebergs

People love to argue.
About the best song Jelly Roll wrote.

Some people say it is BURNIN' THE ICEBERG.
Others say BIG FOOT HAM.
Turtles say TURTLE TWIST.

Sea Life

I say: is it true that Jelly Roll loved turtles?
Or maybe he ate them.
People used to eat turtles.
Even in cartoons.

Police Sketch

Front teeth bad.
Bow tie.
Nice smile.
Bumptious.

Everybody!

Everybody has a godmother.
But only Jelly Roll had an Echo

For a godmother. She said:
Hello, my name is Echo. And

Jelly Roll, child,
I love you.

PLOT SYNOPSIS OF EARTH VS. THE SPIDER
 (American International Pictures, 1958)

Jack Flynn is driving down a highway at night, looking at
a bracelet he has bought his daughter on her birthday.
Suddenly he hits something and his vehicle crashes.
The next morning, his teenage daughter Carol is concerned
her father didn't come home the night before.
She convinces her boyfriend Mike to assist in a search
for her father. They find his crashed truck and the bracelet,
but not his body. Thinking he crawled into a nearby cave,
they investigate.

(So far, no spider.)

STILL, IT'S NICE TO BE KISSED

They say kisses sweeter than wine but most wine —
particularly good red wine — let's say from Burgundy —
and now I am thinking specifically of *Domaine de La
Romanee-Conti* in Vosne whose wines often run more
than five hundred dollars a bottle and there is a very
small supply available of these wines every year in spite
of the exorbitant price — is not at all sweet, in fact, you
might even call it earthy, loamy, with hints of moss and
black tea and tobacco leaf, or as the French might suggest,
of redolent *terroir,* quite delicious, yet, in fact, bone-dry.

BLACK BLUE JEANS, NOIR

You can buy jeans that are black but don't call them black jeans.
Call them: jeans that are black, or jeans of the night.

I SEE YOU BENEATH THE COVERS

In the middle of the earth you are in outer space.
You are asleep and snoring sweetly.

THE TRUTH IS SOMEWHERE IN BETWEEN

Fiction writers write: "It rained today."
Non-fiction writers write: "It did not rain today."

THE ROAD LESS TRAVELLED

When the volume knob broke on my television,
I fell in love with what I thought people were
saying on TV.

THE FUN THING ABOUT BEING IN HEAVEN & MONA LISA

The people you knew only from paintings are now walking
around and eating sandwiches and dancing and laughing
and patting you on the butt.

BOXING

Is being hit in the face by people whom you don't know
or sometimes people you do know who sometimes
like you. I wonder how many boxers say "I'm sorry"
when they hit the other boxers in the face.

The best boxers say "Don't worry, it's fine"
when they get hit in the face. But these are the old
fashioned boxers. They're courtly and gallant.
Their gloves were huge and the color of the ocean at night.

Now these boxers are telling stories to little boys and girls.
The boys and girls are mesmerized. "Is that true?"
they'll ask, trembling. "No," they say with a smile,
"These things I am telling you –
 they never really happened."

CHAPTER TWO

My mother was older when she had me, and she used to tell me
that she was worried that even though she was certain
that she had happy memories, she couldn't remember them.
And so when I was a very little boy, she bought me a small
blue diary and instructed me to write down my happy
memories in it every day, without fail, and I did. I started
in the morning after I woke up, and then before breakfast,
and then after breakfast, and then during school at recess,
and then after school, and then before dinner, and then after
dinner, and then just before I said my prayers and then before
and after I read a story and then right before I went to bed.
And every time I wrote about my happy memories I always
wrote the same happy memory: "writing."

MY FIRST WIFE

Shari was a puppeteer on television in 1963
and she had an adorable puppet named LAMB CHOP
who could scrunch up his face in a really cute way and

also a puppet named CHARLIE HORSE who was also cute
and mischievous too and when I watched Shari and Lamb Chop
and Charlie Horse I felt like they were all my friends

but Shari was not just my friend Shari was so pretty and
Shari's voice was so beautiful I wanted her to be my wife
and I figured we could live in a small cabin with pretty green

fields and corn growing everywhere near the cabin where
Lassie and her family lived nearby and they could be our neighbors
and we could have bonfires and roast weenies on bonfires

but when 1964 came it was an election year, and
election night, and on that night everyone wondered
who would be President: would it be Lyndon B Johnson

or would it be Barry Goldwater and the television station
took all the old Shari and Lamb Chop and Charlie Horse
tapes and everything they did on those tapes and put them into

their television taping machines and taped that long night
that seemed to last forever with the Shari and Lamb Chop
tapes but when the night ended Lyndon B Johnson won and

he was very happy and later he would do some good things
and some bad things too and Barry Goldwater lost and he was
sad but he was also pretty scary and if you look closely at that

tape you can see Barry Goldwater saying I am sorry I lost
and it is so loud you can barely hear him but Shari, my wife,
she was so beautiful back then that you can practically still

see her on tape behind Barry and look what she's doing
she's kissing Lamb Chop right on the lips and Lamb Chop
is blushing and saying *awww* and Barry Goldwater is saying

awww too and things would never be the same again
for me or for Lamb Chop or for Barry Goldwater or

for Lassie or the pretty green fields or corn or anybody
else I ever knew or met or wished I had met and loved
and loved and loved

MERCY

Swimming, my hand disconnects water from water.
I know the feeling of being broken in half.
It's a good feeling.
You get to see yourself go away.
You, just like you,
Watch you.

BLOSSOMS

I change the picture in my wallet frequently.
Right now I have a picture of a cow in a tree.
It is a beautiful Japanese cherry tree that
blossoms in April, and bears fruit in July.
This photograph was taken in October.
The leaves of the tree are golden, and
it was a beautiful day. I must mention
that the cow in the tree is an ordinary cow,
of plastic. His coloring is black and white.
He is about the size of a child's fist.
He is smiling, which cows can do
but it is not always obvious.
With this cow, it is more obvious
than with most cows, for this cow
appears to be resting comfortably
in the cherry tree. Winter will soon
be here, for the cow and the cherry tree.
Everyone loves winter. Cherry trees, in winter,
are beautiful, and the cow is happy now, and
will be happy later. Of all the photographs
I have had in my wallet, this one...

MY NEW PARAGRAPH

I wrote an entire paragraph about my experience
in the barber shop today.

It was a very pleasant experience and I wanted
to tell everyone I knew about it.

Once I had written it, I erased it. Even though
the experience in the barber shop

was wonderful, and writing about the barber shop
was wonderful, what I wrote

was not; it was feeble. It was not fair, I felt, to write
about a wonderful experience

feebly. Suddenly, something happened to my pencil.
And so what I have left is this:

My barber's name is Bradley.
He cuts his wife's hair.
He loves his wife.
He has brown hair.
He has two children.
And a mustache.

My pencil.

WHATEVER HAPPENED TO MR. GREEN JEANS?

He died, during the Reagan Administration.

SURVEY OF CHILDREN DRAWING
THE ATOM BOMB IN 1953

Some have blond hair.
Some have brown hair.
Some have brownish hair.
Some have orange hair.
(Or as some might call it: red.)

SURVEY OF CHILDREN
WHO ARE JUST DRAWING
IN GENERAL

Some have glasses.
Some do not.
Some have pencils.
Some have crayons.
With which they are drawing.
None have mustaches.

SURVEY OF CHILDREN IN GENERAL

Eating Peanut Butter & Jelly.
Looking for meteors.
Eating cheese straws.
Looking for horses to draw.
Drinking wax bottle candy juice.

SURVEY OF PEOPLE WATCHING
COMING ATTRACTIONS

Some are on their phones.
Some are crying.
Some are trying to eat their popcorn.
Some are having trouble with their Tootsie Roll wrappers.
Some have mustaches.
Some of them are saying I hate coming attractions.
One is waving at me.

SURVEY OF PEOPLE WALKING
TOWARDS SUPER TARGET

There are 50 people an hour.
They are all walking quickly.
Except one man who is explaining
baseball to a boy.
The boy is walking quickly.
He has to walk quickly.
Everyone else walks slowly.

SURVEY OF PEOPLE MAKING LOVE
IN WHITE OAK APARTMENTS
ON FRIDAY NIGHT

Apt. A-14.
Apt. I-19.
Apt. B-7.
Apt. B-29 (and 28)
~~Apt. B-40~~ (She was just tossing and turning)

SURVEY OF PEOPLE EATING OUTSIDE

Some are swatting mosquitos.
Some are looking at mosquitos.
Some are saying "Without a bun please."
Some are saying "With a bun please."
Some look like Joseph Zawinul.
Some look like Wayne Shorter.
Some are thinking: where is my food?
Some are say grace.

SURVEY OF A THERMOMETER

It reads 81.
It reads 95.
It has blue ink.
It has red ink.
It was made in Ohio.

A man name Phil made it.
It reads 96.

SURVEY OF A DESK

It has a Slinky on it.
Slinky is a wonderful toy.
If you are nervous it's nice to have a Slinky.

SURVEY OF A DINING ROOM TABLE

It has a gardenia on it.
The gardenia is in a can of tangerine juice.
It has six candles on it.
It has a little basket on it.
It has a jar of honey in the basket.
It has a ticket to Lincoln Center in the basket.
Beethoven is looking at the table.
GI Joe is looking at the table.
It has a woman cut in half on it.

SURVEY OF A DONKEY IN A FIELD

He is wandering.
He has nothing to do.
He has no donkey friends.
Wait.
Here comes a girl
with apples and carrots.
In a big bucket.

GLASS HALF FULL

If you are the Invisible Man, you don't have to say I Love You all the time.

TOMORROW NEVER KNOWS

I have never been happy or sad buying Scotch tape.
Which is why when people ask: "When you die,
what would you like to come back as?
I almost always say: "Scotch tape."
Although sometimes, if I am in the right mood,
I say: "Anything but Scotch tape."

REMOTE CONTROL

SIngle people watch old TV shows when they eat dinner
and so they have many different families. They don't get
along with everyone in their families, but who does?

It's wonderful to be able to choose a family to suit your mood.
And to choose the old chestnuts that you want to see again.
You can even adjust the volume, and even listen again to anything
you want to, or stop whenever you don't want to hear something

Being said. And once you have bought a television set, it doesn't
cost a thing. Is there anything sad about that? Not that I can think of.
And if you think there is, I have no control of that.

Single people watch old TV shows when they eat dinner.
Sometimes this happens, even on old TV shows.

THE FUTURE OF RED FLAGS

In this dream there is no traffic.
And the asphalt is made of ice.
Which is not scary when you think about it.

But if someone else has my dream
they will say there is traffic.
They will be afraid.

There's a boy out there.
They will say. A boy.
A boy on the ice.

A SERIOUS ONE, NOT LIKE FRED GWYNNE'S

If I hold my mouse at just the right angle
I can see a little flashing red light on the *limonata*
soda can. A timid gardenia leaf rests in *limonata*

the flashing red light looks like a police car
and when I see the light I think to myself:

I must go to church more often
one so close that it is not far away
I like things best when they are empty
and near

MOCK APPLE PIE

So in the matter of a few short years
The Ritz modified its surroundings
until it was a mock apple pie.

I know you are thinking:
"It's a hotel" – well, it's really
a pie that used to be a hotel,
and inside of it are no apples
but it is quite crunchy and
elegant in taste – it is tasty

I want you to think about how
lucky you are to have lived
when you did.

Once, people
would simply eat pies
and not hotels.

You had both.

You remember when

Everyone wore a hat.

Everyone was lucky.

And everyone was

Filled with pie.

WHAT'S SURPRISING ABOUT A BELL

If you want it to make noise, you have to let it go and strike it. If you want it to be silent, you must hold it in place to be silent.

WEATHER REPORT

If you desire someone, you never say "I desire you"
because all of your energy is wrapped up in desire
including the part that makes words so you just say
sounds like the grunty sounds you hear in the ocean
at night when a hurricane is coming and you are sleeping.
Part of you is a little awake then, dreaming of your hurricane –
how it comes and goes

A GLOBE OF SWEET WATER

I order almost everything I want from a shop in Indiana.
And so I think of Indiana as a really beautiful and exotic
place that has everything one might want in it. When
I place my orders to Indiana, they receive the orders
and then contact a number of different places around
the world: Tokyo, Munich, London, Hong Kong, etc.,
and ask them for the products that I want. These places
all know each other and are quite something in their own
right but what they really have in common is that they all
know Indiana – and they think of Indiana as a place that
is really beautiful and exotic, and also very worldly and
with an extraordinary sense of connections all around
the world. If only they knew that Indiana was not only
a place but a man: six feet tall and handsome, with
a broad mustache and a fresh smack of bay rum
on his cheeks. I saw him recently sporting
a tan umbrella, which for him was quite unusual.
He comes from Indiana and therefore is Indiana;
he is everything Indiana is and is not.

LASSIE COME HOME

There goes the coffee on the stove again!
I feel like it is trying to tell me something.
Perhaps Billy is trapped in the old mine shaft.

THE ARCHEOLOGY OF ROCK

The point of going to a rock n roll club is to look
at the musicians you see on stage and try to figure
out which ones are married. Once you have decided,
you look at their fingers and see if they are wearing
rings. If you are wrong, you can say *Darn It!*

They say it is easy to guess but I don't think that's true
but that's what I hear. And it's much easier to know
for sure with guitarists than it is with drummers,
that's because drummers' hands are moving very fast.
Guitarists hands move fast, too, but it's over a much
more limited amount of space. Drummers hands move,
but so do their arms and even their legs.

Drummers' arms are almost always thin.
And so are guitarists's arms.

Guitarists move their heads.
Singers move their legs and hips.

Everyone wears sunglasses at midnight.

It doesn't matter if they're married.

SCIENCE TV

The tides are easier to predict than the weather because the number of forces acting upon them are limited and consistent; the number of forces acting upon the weather are infinite and variable. This is why I have always found tides boring, and the weather fascinating. Given the choice, though, I would live with the tides. And eventually I would drown of course, and become part of the weather.

IMPULSE PULSE WHEN I WENT TO PARIS

I bought an oboe in Paris for $900 because
it's nice to think that someday I might learn how
to play the oboe in Paris with an oboe from Paris.

NOTE LEFT TO MY HONEY

If you ever come to earth, you won't find me,
because I will be out looking for you.

A MEMORY OF LOVE

Is like a newspaper. I only say this because a newspaper can be so many things, often helpful and kind.

COMFORT ZONE

Al Capone's jail cell had a Wooton desk
and a reading chair and two lamps, one
with fringe, an oriental rug and a ballerina
sculpture atop a console radio. The plaster
was chocolate-colored and falling off the wall
onto the couch which was covered with a red cloth.
There was a painting, perhaps of a dog, a small plant
on a pedestal, a thin, narrow skylight, and a ghost —
his name was James, but everyone called him Jim
or Jimbo.

100 YEAR OLD BOX OF NEGATIVES DISCOVERED
FROZEN IN BLOCK OF ANTARCTICA'S ICE

Contained images of men wearing long coats, walking on ice.

WRITING STYLE

If you are in a room, look at anything in the room.
Look really hard until you see a frame around it.

WHERE IS THAT WAVE

I think about that wave that was right in front of me
in the bay when I was six years old and standing on
the dock on a rock and learning how to fish and
it was early in that morning and this morning I say:
where that wave is now? Where IS that wave?

LOVE AND CAVES

I knew exactly what a cave was like before I ever went
into one. Picture books are so great because they make
you feel these things before you ever do them or know
them and when you do, it comes as no surprise and it is
exactly as you imagined it to be. But come to think of it,
I have never been in a cave. I wonder what it is like.
It probably feels like no surprise at all or maybe it does
and there you are walking around in it and saying
"this is wonderful and not at all what I thought
it would be" – but still, a delightful thing.

ACTION ADVENTURE

Someone once described cotton candy as sweet spun glass
and I never ate it again because I didn't want to hurt myself,
which is strange, since I don't really enjoy a movie unless
at least two people jump through windows and glass goes
flying everywhere. But to be fair, I want them to then
get up and brush themselves off and be perfectly fine.

But sometimes after the glass, they fight.

HISTORY CLASS

I shouldn't judge the years I don't know personally.

THE REAL NAME OF THE A & P

was: "The Atlantic & Pacific Tea Company."
When I read its name I wanted to drink tea.
And so I started drinking tea. And then I moved
to the South and started to drink sweet tea.
And then I felt sick and the doctor said:
"You've got kidney stones and you have to
stop drinking sweet tea." But before I did
I married a girl named Ida. I think of Ida now,
her face covered with funnel cake, her lips
so tender, underneath a summer moon
like Beth before her, her neck so white and soft.

MY FAVORITE STORY ABOUT AUSTRALIA
AFTER THE GREAT WAR USING THE PASSIVE VOICE

In the late 1960's Wham-O made a "giant" Super Ball,
roughly the size of a bowling ball, as a promotional stunt.
It fell from the 23rd story window (some reports say the roof)
of an Australian hotel and destroyed a parked convertible car
on the second bounce.

MR. BRENNAN

Walter Brennan was an actor who appeared to be

much older than he actually was.

This made it easier for him to work in movies.

Especially Westerns.

Where you wear big hats.

He was a lovable curmudgeon.

I think men liked him.

I bet Gary Cooper liked him.

I don't know what women thought of him.

Like Gertrude Stein.

I think he was just fine.

Because he was often in Westerns and he often wore a hat.

Except that he mumbled and dagnabbit'd a lot when he talked.

And because he mumbled and dagnabbit'd

it is always really hard to understand him

when you get older, and your hearing gets worse.

and the first person you can't understand anymore

is Walter Brennan.

You would like to stay but you have to say goodbye

to Walter Brennan.

You have no other choice.

Au Revoir, Mr. Brennan!

Mr Brennan says *Au Revoir!*

I can't call him "Walter."

It would be disrespectful.

Unless of course someday

when I, too, am old

I marry

Mr. Brennan.

TV

The deceased had a light breakfast
of toast and kumquat jelly with tea

and I said to myself:

I think I am going to like
this thing

SURVEY OF JAPAN

One tsunami

Many ghosts

Many taxi cabs

Seven ghosts in cabs

Cabs without ghosts

Water

. .

SURVEY OF MUSIC IN 1967

Pillows

Fudge

Velvet

Doors

Prunes

Faces

Gravy

Clambake

Gears

Bathing

Tangerine

Honey

Magic

Trogglodynamite

. .

SURVEY OF BACON

Francis

Sir Francis

Maple-cured

SURVEY FOOTNOTE:
THE NEW BIOGRAPHY OF FRANCIS BACON, pg. 1

Few of us found it odd when we first ate bacon,
but Sir Francis Bacon found it very odd indeed.

SUMERIAN PROVERBS FOUND ON A HOT DAY AFTER A TRIP
TO THE GROCERY STORE FOR TUNA FISH & CRACKERS
("History Begins at Sumer" by Samuel Noah Kramer, 1959)

Hygiene
Everybody talks to the well-dressed man.
Except for Fred.

Irony of the Glasses
If I wore glasses, I could see the rich man
and marry him, but I cannot afford glasses.

A Shrine and a River
My wife is in the outdoor shrine.
My mother is in the river.
Is she naked?
I am starving from hunger.
And yet I have a wife and a naked mother.

Bereft
He who has never had a wife or a child
has never owned a leash although he might
own a dog or a wolverine or perhaps a whirligig.

Plentitude
A frisky woman can take pain
and add a dollop of ache to it
Who knows where she finds it?
But she does because of her
energy which is quite abundant
but not good and she is a good shopper
she loves going out in the evenings

Inquiry of Self
I am a steed
tied to a mule
who must draw a cart
who hates mules.

Memories

In my cart
are not riches
just stupid things
reeds and stubble
for example
from my master's yard
and beard, respectively.

Bonds

Friendship lasts a day
but if you love someone
you will not die until they do
or vice versa and so forth and so on.

Labour

The blacksmith's dog overturns the flower pot for he
cannot overturn the anvil for he is a weak, bad dog.

Immortality

After escaping the wild ox
The wild cow asked me if I was OK
I said yes and then
the wild bull gored me post haste
These are my last words
I just wanted you to know them.

Greed

He longs to catch the fox and make it into a stole
He already imagines it around his neck
while the fox imagines marrying and settling down
with a beautiful woman in a house built of pine needles.

Morals

I snuck onto my neighbor's property and stole his house
and while I did my neighbor snuck onto my property and
stole my house

My mother was naked in the river, still.

THE CRITTER CATCHER

With a gentle sucking motion, the Critter Catcher sweeps up a spider with its soft nylon bristles and holds him fast. Who do you want to be when you grow up? I want to be that spider, saying *woo woo*.

THE FRESH DONUTS OF LAUNDRY in SPACE

There is a two week window in the summer when
tomatoes are perfect.

A firefly is perfect in a smaller window.

In the photograph, the window isn't made of glass.

I see you waving in a window of glass.

I enjoy breaking nothing but still
I can't help it

I want to look
at the glass

TIME LAPSES IN NEW ENGLAND

I've always liked John Quincy Adams' house before there were
cars in front of it, when the road was barely paved, when
there were only a few trees behind it, when the stone wall

        encircled it, when there was no traffic light
        in front of it, and on a day like Tuesday when
        John Quincy Adams would walk out the front door

and say, "What a beautiful morning! If only I didn't have
to work on the Monroe Doctrine today" and then sigh
and go out and work on the Monroe Doctrine

        but only after a refreshing skinny dip in a pond
        that you can't see John Quincy Adams naked in,
        anymore.

THISTLE

A girl who grew up in the ocean
and then came to America
to purchase with delight
a red velvet chapeau.

VOCATION VS STYLE

JOE'S PIZZA
About 3,850,000 results (0.55 seconds)

JOE'S PIZZAZZ
About 85,000 results (0.47 seconds)

BLENDER

I find myself more and more empathetic towards inanimate objects
as I grow older. This morning as I washed the hand blender,
I thought to myself: "Poor blender, what a life he leads."
Some might say that the blender has a life of purpose, but at
what cost? Still, I only find myself feeling empathetic towards
the blender when I am making pancakes or chocolate chip cookies.
Some might say that this is the one time that I *shouldn't* feel sorry
for the blender, or that I shouldn't worry about such things, or that
I should think about the blender more often, although few people
I know say that thing, but they are adamant about it when they do.

THE CHOICES OF CRAYOLA

The Crayon maker used to make rubber for car tires
before he made crayons, but Elsa didn't care and
she was drawing a duck. A duck who was about to be
hit by a car, and the car was colored in thistle, maize,
and raw umber, and the duck, oh the duck was only
white, a lot of white, with a little lemon-yellow on top –
a touch of spring-green beneath its tires.

ICÉPHORE NIÉPCE

Part of me wants to be one of those photogravures you find
at antique shops – of people who no one remembers but
seem to be so nice, from so long ago.

Part of me wants to see those photogravures walking down
the street and stopping them to say: "Don't I know you?"

Part of me wants to be the man who invented the photogravure
on the day he sat down to eat a bowl of ice cream and thought
to himself: "It's awfully hot today, too hot to photogravure."

And to be all the people who passed by and escaped that day,
like wee-tender baby ghosts.

REVELATORY

I haven't been able to read without glasses for ten years, but today I went outside and picked up a magazine and read it perfectly. *Hoorah!* I said. *I don't need my glasses ever again!* And so I took them off, and threw them into the Van Hootens' pool.

I LOVE THIS PICTURE OF THIS RECORD

The name of this record is:
HOW A LITTLE GIRL
LIKE YOU COULD LOVE ME
and it is played by
Lloyd Dayton & His Music.

The color of this record
is a combination of green
and black. Here are some
of the words you can find
on this record:

"Electric Record"; "REGAL" (big letters);
"Lloyd Dayton & his Music"; "10184B";
"Dick Dixon"; "Vocal Chorus."

Also, you can find the words "Fox Trot":
I think this is in case you are buying a record
that you are not familiar with, and let's say
you want to fox trot, you know that this is
a record to which you can fox trot were you
to purchase it. Which isn't to say you could buy
a record that didn't say "Fox Trot" on it and not
dance a fox trot to it, but this at least helps you
to fox trot to a song that is a fox trot kind
of song.

Of course, how many fox trot people are there these days?
Not many I guess. I was at a retirement home recently,
and I was thinking about this, and there was a woman in a
wheelchair down the hall, a very nice lady, and I asked if if
she ever foxtrotted when she was a little girl, and she said
Heavens no, I did not, and then she told me how old she
was, and she was five years younger than me, and I thought

to myself, My God, I am getting old, I better learn how to
fox trot before it is too late, but then again, I thought to
myself, it probably is too late already, which for some
reason made me happy, or maybe I just felt relieved,
and I left the retirement home and drove to my house
and went to bed but couldn't sleep but later could and
when I did I was dancing in my sleep.

AND THIS

This record here is small and round
and the title of the record is:
SUSIE, SUSIE, WHY WON'T
YOU MARRY ME? and it was

performed by the Six Black
Diamonds and it even has a
Spanish translation
beneath the title

(SUSIE, SUSIE, ¿POR QUÉ
NO TE CASAS CONMIGO?)
and it was made in 1926.
My guess is that Susie did not

marry him because she did not
love him. Most people do not marry
other people because they do not love them.

Sometimes they marry them anyway just to be polite.
Sometimes they don't marry and they just don't know
why, even when they are asked politely they don't know
what to say. In this case, If the man who wanted to marry

Susie were 20 years old in 1926 and asking Susie
to marry him then, he would now be 110 years old
and a widower if he were still alive and if Susie loved
him and married him and died, and he would now be
a single man if he were still alive if Susie did not love him
and did not marry him, regardless of whether or not she
was alive herself. So eventually love becomes a matter
of semantics because no matter what you do it ends up
pretty much the same and so it isn't something that should
worry you too much. Still, it is interesting that in Spanish,

the word for marriage is almost the same as the command:
make me a house!

Susie, Susie, why do you not make me a house?

SINCE WE ALL DIE, WHY DO WE HAVE PEOPLE DIE (IN THE MOVIES?)

My favorite squares are the ones you see on the trampoline
as you are about to touch it with your feet.

My favorite circles are the circles that are made by
Vitamin B6 tablets.

My favorite pens are the fuzzy topped ones that look like
ice creams cones if you see their shadows on the wall.

My favorite grandfathers are the ancient grandfathers from
Constantinople or the fuzzy haired rock stars from the '70's
when they become grandfathers after they settle down.

My favorite name is Vitalis.

My favorite smell is Vitalis.

My favorite crutches are made of maple wood
and smell and sound like breakfast cereals with milk.

My favorite guns are ones that are owned by people named Ed.

My favorite color is Tutti Frutti, said really slowly.

My favorite candy bar was made by the Mennonites
in the 17th century and consisted mostly of flax seed
and millet and apples and hominy and special secret ingredients.

My favorite time is the time you find on a clock.

My favorite lock is made out of hair that looks like a real lock.

My favorite church is the one with the tricycles and helmets and boxes of Goobers atop.

My favorite President is George Washington, Senior.

My favorite time to say "Señor" is when I am praying
real loud in a barn.

My favorite peanut butter sandwich has a base note
of cassis and lavender.

My favorite mustache is chopped off and in a box
labeled "fresh minnows"

My favorite perfume says *Parfum* on it.

My favorite music I can't tell you about.

My favorite Atom Bomb was in a cartoon.

My favorite word is *why not.*

My favorite wrecking ball is made of peppermint. And steel.

My favorite place in heaven is the gift shop.

My favorite termite dances just like Christopher Walken.

SKYDIVER WHO ATTEMPTS JUMP WITHOUT PARACHUTE...

Sometimes I just read the first half of a headline.
And then I go into the kitchen and have a glass of milk
and read the funnies. Oh. I also whistle a little
and I am pouring the milk now.

.

GIVE ME YOUR TOAST

It is impossible to say that there is no life on other planets.
It is possible to say "There is." You can say: "There is
life on other planets" much as you might say: "There is
toast on your plate" and then: "Give me your toast"
and then: "I want your toast." But this would be rude
to say in the *extremis* but it would be possible.
On other planets, it might not be rude at all.
On other planets, it might not be possible to say
"I want your toast" because there is no oxygen
in the atmosphere, nor is there atmosphere,
nor is there toast on the plate on the table
although it is comforting to know
there is a plate, and that beneath that plate
is a table, and that table is not floating, it is
quite still and it is time for breakfast on
a new planet. You however, are floating.
As am I. Eating breakfast. Biscuits, mostly,
in my beautiful house.

PURPLE CAR

*The Whole Time I Had a Friend Named Franz
Franz Liszt Never Crossed My Mind*

I wish I had a purple car
because it would look so good
as I drove by holding a lemon sherbet cup

People would say: "That's a delightful combination!"
while others might throw their undergarments in joy

Just like they did in the days of Franz Liszt (ca. 1800
something.) But not at everybody. Only at Franz.
That sexy man simply knew how to rock a piano

like a little God. If you don't believe me, look it up.
Garments were thrown. Ladies fainted.

Blows were exchanged. Blow jobs were exchanged.
A glove was lost. A glove of Franz. *Un Petit Dieu!*

If I am wrong, you can punch me in the face.
If I am right, you can punch me in the face anyway.

Sometimes I feel like my face could
use a good punch. After all, what have I done

in this life, other than imagine purple and lemon
together, tell you my little stories, with as you were
and I as I was and why – nothing else

If only I could play the piano
like Franz Liszt before he died
and lost one glove
and then another

PUNY THINGS MAKE ME FEEL MIGHTY

Why do I feel patient with an ant
and less so with this fellow who is
driving a small car from Yugoslavia
in an interesting fashion on the road
but not in the fashion that I might drive
a car from Japan were I to do that

How do I know? I have owned a car
from Japan and I drove it. Once the door
went flying open and someone almost
screamed, but now they are asleep. Once
I told a funny joke in a car from Yugoslavia –
we laughed and laughed and then
someone made a squeaky sound. Now
they live in Ireland and drink Stout
and wear festive underwear.

Such exciting moments bring back
many memories, not all of them good.
Some of them, yes, good. Now.
Back to the ant.

For me, it is quite easy
to be patient with an ant.

GOOD MORNING

When someone says *Hello, Sunshine*
I wonder if they truly know
the awesome power of the sun
and how afraid they should be of it
and how they should run from it
as fast as they can

For sunshine is a powerful thing
that you should fear and that
you should hide from and that
you should never say hello to.

I like to say hi
to cloudy days and small caves
in small, lush countries.

JFK

In the photograph, five small children
are standing outside a clapboard house
next to a clothesline and beneath a window

that is open in summer. If they fell asleep
in the sun and woke up eighty years later,
they would be standing next to the runway

at the JFK airport and two cars would be
honking and telling the elderly to get out
of the road because, naturally, they are late

for their flight and time is money. By then
they would be too old to move like they once
did and they would get upset and they would cry

and they would miss their old house. Only a special
airplane can take you there, a voice would say, coming
from the open window on a summer day. But that airplane,
he has hidden away. He is a bad, bad Daddy.

CREST

Blue is the right color for a toothpaste
for it is the color of the Aegean Sea
Crayola Crayon

A PREFERENCE FOR SWANS over OTHERS

There are geese outside my office building, and because I grew up in the city
I never knew how nasty a goose could be, but believe me, geese are nasty,
they want to do terrible things to you, and they aren't afraid to say so, and
there is a faint aspect of desperation to their actions, and I should perhaps
feel sorry for them because of the highway, and the cars, but also I have to go
to work, to get into my office building, and so I would rather think about swans

and swan boats, and that beautiful lake with the swans,
and a soft breeze, and their magnificent swan color, and
the gentle way they have with their babies, and so I recline
under a small tree near the office building and rest my eyes
and think about swans, swans and more swans and all swans
until the geese come and do whatever they want to do
to me – and do things they do – I don't want to think
about that. I prefer thoughts of swans, and swans, and soon,
when the morning has gone and the geese have done
whatever it is that they do, I will prefer swans even more.

SPURNED

I saw a bottle cap.
But I saw no bottle.
How lonely the bottle cap.
How dare the bottle.

INSOMNIA IN THE MOUNTAINS

I hate the balloon rubbing sound
that is produced by thinking

À LA RUSSE

Enjoy my fedora
said the fedora maker
to the man who loved fedoras
at the fedora shop
who almost bought
a fedora
for his wife
to give him
for she loved fedoras
when he wore them
and then she went
to buy another
for him with which
to love him more
than ever and then
she was hit

by a bus and
the bus driver
had no hat

NINETEEN FIFTY-SEVEN

Some Chevys were the color of swimming pools.
Some Chevys were the color of plush seats in movie theaters.
Some Chevys were the color of a lemon sherbet.
Some Chevys were the color of a plate of peas.
Some Chevys were the color of a whiff of sea foam.
Some Chevys were red.

LIFE IN THE FUNNIES

His yellow hair was easy to explain.
He drew a picture of himself when he was seven
and has kept it in his pocket ever since.

NOT SUPERMAN

I was the only one on the dance floor
but that didn't stop me from dancing
like a fool with my imaginary girlfriend
to the funky beat of the band inside
my head until I was overwhelmed
with desire for a real glass
of water poured into my real glass
by someone real
like for instance
oh let's say
Clark Kent

BRIQUETTES

No, there is no better word in the world.
People keep trying, and people keep
demuring to the champ. Only the French
dare to disagree, and Frenchily so, for in
their possession is: *dénouement,* and
dénouement, they possess it gleefully,
as one might possess a poodle or a push toy,
and with the commensurate joy.

Yet is it a viable contender?
I say: put *dénouement*
on the fire, and let's find out.

PETER LORRE FLUBS THE AUDITION

I love the headline, so much in fact, that I don't read the story.
I want to think of Peter Lorre and all the different ways that
he might have flubbed the audition. I want to think about
these things because Peter Lorre is such a great actor
I can't imagine that he ever flubbed the audition.
Although he might have been very young at the time.
Or they might have asked him to use an accent which
was an uncomfortable fit. Or perhaps he wore shoes
with large heels because he wanted to appear
more commanding and it is so difficult to walk
that way. Or perhaps they asked him to dance
and he was wearing his commandingly-heeled shoes.
Perhaps they asked him to perform an act of *jui jitsu*,
but wait, he could perform an act of *jiu jitsu*. Perhaps
he had a cold, or whooping cough. Perhaps he was allergic
to the makeup or it was pollen season. Perhaps his heart
was broken, and he didn't see the point of doing an awesome audition.
Perhaps the director was mean, or he fell down on the ice and hurt
his knee the week before in Vienna. Perhaps he drank too much Sanka
the night before and had trouble sleeping. Is it hard to sleep if you drink
Sanka? Would a man of Peter Lorre's stature drink Sanka?
When was Sanka discovered on this earth?
Was it somewhere else before this?
I must research that.

Peter Lorre flubbed the audition.

I SAW HER ACROSS THE ROOM

Apple with melted chocolate.
Peanut butter and drizzled coconut.
Marshmallow *crème* and sprinkles.

NICE SNAPSHOT

There were a thousand times I could have met her
Why did I wait until the last time before I did?

ACTION

Vvedensky said that we go together
like a barn owl and an owl.
Didn't he mean a barn owl and a barn?
I didn't like the idea of a barn owl and an owl.
And so I smooshed it with my thumb.
The same thumb I used for smooshing stamps
on letters. And then I wrote you a letter about
an owl and a barn, called "Barn, The Owl."

I was the owl.
We were the barn owl.
The barn was no longer
important. The letter
was never sent.

WHY DID I GROW UP WASTING SO MUCH TIME FEARFUL
OF SKUNKS WHO WOULD SPRAY ME IN THE FACE?

A family of skunks came up to me and sniffed my shoes
and they wiggled their noses and then they sniffed my bike.
And then they say *Au Revoir,* and scuttled down the road and
into a clump of bushes making little chirpy sounds and so on.

This is what I did today instead of that.

SILVER

Mostly we like to go to movies filled with actors younger
than we are and say

How terribly old they look! Don't they look terribly old?
Much older than we do!

And then we go out for ice cream and postcards of
a hundred year old tree

that looks younger than we do, and we are only five
but we don't mind! We are sitting underneath

that old tree, kissing like time forgot us.

THE LAST BUS

The last bus leaves at 8:00 and the bus stop is right in front
of the realty shop. One day I decided to buy a house, and now
I think of its embers every time I stand waiting for a bus in front
of the flower shop.

NOTHING AND NOWHERE

There is nothing like a chocolate malted milkshake
after a good rock concert. But all the milkshake joints
are closed! What do we do? We go to the cheesecake
stores, instead, and ask them: "Do you have chocolate
malted milkshakes?" and they say:

"No, you should try the milkshake joints" and we say
"We did!" and they say "How about a cheesecake?"
and we say "Why not?" and they say "Coming right up!"
and we say "Great!" and run out the door like naked people.

SON OF A BRIEF ENCOUNTER

Every time I buy a ticket, I am giving money to someone whose name I do not know, and who has lived a life that I only know the smallest conceivable part of.

DODGE BALL 1 through 4

I wake up every day, and think about what it was like to play dodge ball when I was seven. And then I play dodge ball. I am eight.

I have been playing dodge ball wrapped in nostalgia. Much as one might wrap a hot dog in aluminum foil from a place far away and long ago according to your mother's mother's mother.

Those who cannot play Dodge Ball
are those who are not acquainted
with the term Dodge Ball.
All others can play Dodge Ball.

Once, in a dream, I confused Dodge Ball with Red Rover.
When I awoke, the room was filled with doctors and nurses
saying: *It's a boy!*

MILK

is a miracle. Don't ever let anyone tell you differently.
Tasty, rich, satisfying, and the color of a blinding snowstorm.
Chocolate milk is another miracle. Zesty, yummy, perfect –
and the color of ancient pantaloons. Don't listen to people
who say it isn't. They are filled with bitterness and regret.

Hot Cocoa is God.
Chocolate bars, Jesus.

THE KING

Next time you feel a gyration coming on, remember:

In geometry, a gyration is a rotation in a discrete subgroup
of symmetries of the Euclidean plane such that the subgroup
does not also contain a reflection symmetry whose
axis passes through the center of rotational symmetry.

A DOLLOP

When I read that the air rested on the earth,
I stopped feeling sorry for the air, and also,
I stopped feeling sorry for the earth.

100%

Nothing is more satisfying than knowing that.

VISITING JENNIE

It's so nice to have neighbors who know how to cook well
and not poorly when you live in an apartment building if
the building was built either cheaply or hastily, or not out
of brick or something substantial like brick like let's say
a house made in 1920 unless you don't leave the house
much, or unless you leave the house of 1920 by the
back door to see your friend, Jen.

TOURISTY

What excited me most was that the marquee on the restaurant read:
THE WORLD'S FINEST COFFEE. I don't drink coffee. But I do think
about the sort of place that people might go to were they to want to
drink the world's finest coffee. And I think about the man who might
build a restaurant and say that he offers the world's finest coffee, and
I think that taken together this is a very fine combination of things to
consider when it is a cold day and you are in a city that you don't know
very well, and you want to go inside and get warm not only your body
of course, but also your spirit needs a certain goosing and right there
in the middle of the street you see the sign LOU MITCHELL:
THE WORLD'S FINEST COFFEE and so you walk in and stop
for a moment and smell that wonderful smell – what is that?
It's Lou coffee, it must be, and everywhere you see: nice people,
dressed snuggly, looking out at the snow, holding warm white cups.

VARIABLES

I would like a ceramic water cooler
and I would like a small bookshelf
FOR CHRISTMAS

I wish that everyone would get together
and buy them for me. If they did,
I would invite them over for
coffeecake or strudel.

If they didn't, I would invite them over
anyway. They really should buy me
a ceramic water cooler and bookshelf
because clearly I am a nice guy
what with my coffeecake and strudel
and whatnot but not for long will I be

a nice guy It's not like I am going to buy
coffeecake forever. And if I do, and there
is no water cooler and bookshelf,
I will hide it in the backyard

next to the little popsicle stick crosses
shoved deep into the earth next to
the palm tree stub covered in fire ants

TWO SLEEPY PEOPLE

What if two sleepy people got married
in their sleep?

HOTLINE

I water the basil at dawn.
By noon it is not so suicidal.
The phone rings.
I try not to answer it.

INSTRUCTIONS FROM THE TRANSIT AUTHORITY
with Addendum

To travel from UNC Hospitals to Durham in the morning,
use Route 400 or walk to Franklin Street Coffee Shop.
Sit down at the Coffee Shop and have a nice cup of coffee.
Listen to the mockingbirds which frequently dwell in the trees
outside of the Coffee Shop. How melodious they are, how
inviting their song. One of them used to be your girl.

A FRENCHMAN WHOSE LAST NAME BEGINS WITH G

Said that we don't travel in a circular method, but in a spiral,
like a corkscrew, like a corkscrew! Which means that we go
from a high place to a low place swirling, then embedded
in a tree temporarily, until we feel the force of the ages
upon us and then the liberation of sweet perfect aromas
of cedar and mint and plum and cassis or maybe honeysuckle
and kiwi and melon and gooseberry which you are quite near
for a moment but only for a moment, and then we are with
all that one might find in a garbage can: eggs, corned beef hash,
watermelon rinds, chicken fat, cigarette butts, LIFES that were
never read and next there is the quiet, the lack of any real
conversation and then jarring, and tumbling, and travel:
who knows where we are going now? Who cares? it's all so
very spinny and exciting!

EXPLORING THE SIMILE

the movie is over and
I am so hungry that
I could dance like
Fred Astaire
like garlic bits

upon a cast iron
skillet
dance floor

VIRGIN MARY GLUE

I purchased a small plaster statue of the Virgin Mary
twenty years ago

Ten years ago the head fell off and I superglued
the Virgin Mary's head back

onto her neck Rob who helps me fix my bicycle
said that the next time

the Virgin Mary's head falls off that I should use
Gorilla Glue, that Gorilla Glue

is even stronger than Super Glue and Gorilla Glue
will keep the Virgin Mary's head

in place for a nice long time when it falls off again
because Believe me, Rob said, the Virgin Mary's head

will fall off again

RULES OF ORDER

bagpipes are believable
but only when used sparingly
in pornography

SOMEONE STOLE ANNA PAVLOVA'S SLIPPERS

Her ballet slippers and what do you suppose someone is doing with them unless they have feet the size of Anna Pavlova feet that can't dance in them and if they loved them enough to steal them and even if they fit nice and snug they probably aren't dancing with them anyway they love them too much

Anna Pavlova's ballet slippers are in a dusty old shoe box somewhere saying Behold! I am Anna Pavlova's ballet slippers! which you can't hear because of shoebox-tinny voices but they keep saying it anyway they hope something will come of it and they will dance again

which is unlikely, and meanwhile, her regular slippers are under the bed, and the TV is on. At first it's a commercial for cheese snacks, and then a ride in the country in a Chevy, and then it's some evangelist telling us we must pray to God or you just can't imagine the awful, the awful — you just can't imagine.

RETREAT

When the books were removed, the spider scurried
to the corner of the bookcase and curled up into a ball.
As an ostensibly dead spider, surely, no one would kill
her now. She knew if he escaped this mortal fate,
tomorrow she would be capturing flies and eating them
in his bookcase home, *Chez Bookcase*. For now, she would
have to wait. Waiting, they say, is always the hardest part.

UTILITY ONE & TWO

i

The mirror provides you with the opportunity
to see how many times you blink.

ii

The piano can be used as a coffin or
a cooling tray for fudge mint cookies.

SHAME OF THE FLY

I wonder if, before they die, flies are a little embarrassed
that they were caught in a spider web. I imagine it is
much like being pulled over by a state trooper outside
your home or office, when the state trooper approaches
your vehicle with delicate feet, holding a gun or
some sort of fancy spider web.

FRAU IM MOND

On the set of Fritz Lang's silent sci-fi film
«Frau im Mond» 1929

I want to live there but it existed in 1929
and even then it didn't exist

It just sort of 'was' for a little bit of time.

Many people going here and there and
everyone is using a pretend name.

They are all doing things they don't really do.

They are all saying things they never really say.

When someone says "Hello, Bob!"
they are actually talking to Frank.

Or no one at all.

Why, it might even be Bob talking.

There might not even be a Frank.

Bob might be talking to himself.

And the sky isn't even there.

Nor the swirly mountains.

Nor the whirlygigs.

And the dunes are confectionary sugar.

For heaven's sake, let's not talk about the stars.

Let's not talk about this at all.

Seriously.

Let's talk about the future.

This is all about the future.

It's the most wonderful place ever.

I love it with all my heart.

I have had the future for a long time.

And I will love it forever.

And forever I will keep it safe

in my wallet

next to the condoms.

WHY I STOPPED TALKING

Because I heard the garbage truck pull up.
But wait a second! Today's not garbage day!

SATURDAY AFTERNOON

What am I thinking about now? I am thinking about
a hundred children all lined up at a long table
in the middle of a courtyard on a windy day in Rome
just about to eat a hundred bowls of Beefaroni
on a Saturday afternoon and pigeons are flying
gaily above them while I am watching cartoons
in the rec room and the Beatles are in a little garden
in England playing with red guitars, stoned –
1966.

THE STORY OF HEDY LAMARR

Wait. I was going to say something about ants.
What was it? When I see a cockroach, I get angry
and want them to die.

Back to ants: when I see ants, I feel sorry for them.
Their crusades seem so futile. I apologize when I run
cold water over the plate that is filled with ants.

If ants were very large, they would perhaps be frightening.
By "large" I don't mean like the size of a bowling ball or a
suitcase. Let's say the size of a cherry tomato, in season,
fragrant, plump, delicious grilled, with balsamic vinegar
and a little sugar and

Olive oil and pepper, and the ants love three of them on my plate
on the table next to the drawing of Hedy Lamarr. But if they,
the ants, were the size of a tomato, they couldn't eat that
tomato. The ant would know a different sort of suffering

They would run away. And I will be honest, my heart
would break less, if at all, for it. It's important, I tell ants
and friends, to remain modest in your desires, prudent
in your dreams.

IT'S IMPORTANT TO LOVE YOURSELF

But if you do, why would you need anyone else?
You would love someone who loves you.
And you would get married to you

Of course there would be a honeymoon
but eventually things would go south
and you would kick and scream and holler
and you would sleep in separate bedrooms
and you would get a divorce
and be alone again

until you would put you in a rest home
and with a breathe a sigh
you would hold a flower in your hand
turn away from your love
close your eyes forever
and be alone at last

YOU'VE GOT A FRIEND

They said the drug would make me sick to my stomach
but I thought they were kidding they weren't kidding.
Just like when they told me there was no Santa Claus.
Yes. The doctors told me that. They said: "There is
no Santa Claus, buddy" and I smiled because now I had
a buddy, or at least they had me as theirs. 50 years later,
they would say "This drug will make you sick to your
stomach" and I would said "Buddy?" but no: they would
said "Pal."

GOOD FELLAS

In France, you can fish for peaches and it becomes confusing
because peaches and fishing are the same thing. Also: Joe Peche
or *Pesci,* is the same thing as peaches and fishing and original sin.

A steak is not a peach nor is it fishing but it is a sign of
weakness, as it is in the USA. *To go under the peach*
means you are in deep water. *To guard the peach*
means you care for fish and also to care for Joe Peche/

Pesci. *To own a can of peaches* means you employ
a fishing rod. Although you don't have to own it –
you can rent it. *To guard the peach?* It is what you
might think. The best though, is *peach melba:*

It means, simply, peach melba. Better still,
if there is better than best: a peach is an apricot,
only yellow, in Whitehouse, New Jersey.

CLOSE AND PLAY

I wish my father had lived long enough that he could see me type
on a computer and watch the word count change almost as fast
as I type. I think he would have liked it and might have wanted
to do it himself and also might even have been impressed as
he watched me type to see how few spelling errors I made –
it's easy to write perfectly on the computer I would tell him,
and he would listen politely and smooth his hat and tap
his pipe and smile and mumble *hmmpf!*

KUDOS TO JOAN CRAWFORD

For contemplating jumping from a bridge
while wearing a mink stole

THE TWENTIETH CENTURY IN SANDWICHES

(Decades of inception)

1900: peanut butter and jelly

1910: french dip

1920: po' boy

1930: philly steak sandwich

1940: bánh mi

1950: pastrami on rye

1957: I was born

1960: fried chicken sandwich

1970: gyro

1980: panini

1990: wraps

2000: peanut butter and jelly (encore)

ALL CREATURES GREAT AND SMALL

Two small sparrows lifted their heads lazily in the grass when they heard the sound of a bus rumbling nearby. "I have seen a greyhound before, " the smaller sparrow said, "and that's no greyhound." Before the other sparrow could reply, a mustang drove by, breaking, most abruptly, into a foamy gallop.

A JOURNEY TO THE MAILBOX

Oh boy!
A letter from a bank
marked "Private"

GONE

If I had stood at the precise place,
I would have seen your face in every
drop of rain that fell that July.

UNTITLED

I leaned toward her.
She leaned towards me.
And we kissed.

Everyone said what we were doing was wrong.
My head was weary and her hair was blonde.
And we have been married ever since.

Until she died. And Man,
did she die.

JOHNNY CASH & MARILYN MONROE

There's something comforting about looking through famous people's drivers licenses.

I particularly like the parts that say things like: 6' 2" or eyes: blue.

LOVE AND THE DOG WHISTLE

While others could make the sound of a fox walking in
the garden, only she could make the sound of its fur coat.

PAZO

Pazo, they say, makes a complicated Albariño.
He takes a bottle, an ordinary bottle, and fills it
with peaches, lime, hibiscus, slate, flint and pineapple.

But this is not a bottle of Albariño.
And he takes this bottle and smashes it against a ship.

This ship also is not Albariño.
The ship set sail years ago.
Goodbye, ship!

Only Pazo knows the secret of Albariño.
With its heady flavors of peaches, lime,
hibiscus, slate, flint and pineapple.
Albariño is still a ship waiting.

And he knows it has nothing to do with nothing
that he has done so far in his life. Pazo has wasted
his life. He must walk out into the fields. He must
breathe the air. He must meet a girl. He must steal
a grape.

Pazo is a complicated man.
He walks out into the field.
And that's where the police find him.
Flint, and pineapple.

Pazo: is Albariño.

WEATHER REPORT

The leaves forgot to change this year.
They were just too upset at things.

UP AND DOWN

If down goes the airplane
would I clutch the arm of a stranger
and say "I love you"?

I would! And if I did she would say:
"I love you too!" and then she would
say: "I have loved you all my life!"

And then I would say "But we just met!"
And then she would say "True, but..."
— and then we would die.

People are strange.

FANCY PANTS

Salmon Tartare with a dab
of crème fraîche flavored
with fennel and dill

Now here comes the funny part:

resting on a waffle chip

BLUE BOOK

I must inquire:
is a carafe still
an elegant thing?

TWO GUYS FROM MILWAUKEE

is a movie and it's quite rare.
Most movies have three guys
from somewhere.

ANOTHER FINAL SOLUTION

A complicated puzzle
made out of colorful
pieces of candy.

The only way to solve
this puzzle is to eat it.

THE NUTMEG TREE

We stood outside underneath the nutmeg tree.
And when the rain began to fall, it drenched our clothes.
Except for small areas that protected us in the shape of
nutmegs. As we walked out from underneath the nutmeg
tree, it appeared as though we were covered in nutmegs.
Soon, though, it just looked like we were drenched in a way
that almost seemed like autumn. I seem to remember
the rain didn't stop and that year there were nutmegs.

BEING ELDERLY

Each circle is smaller than the last circle
and yet lies outside the previous circle
in a way that makes it hard to draw
or imagine

DEAR JOHN

My favorite days are the ones when the sun comes up and down at the same time. The best part is the booming sound and then the sound of the glass of the stars breaking upon the glass of the earth.

MR. CONGENIALITY

I must stop timing the kisses in Hollywood movies.
So far Lauren Bacall is the winner when she kissed
Kirk Douglas in *Young Man With A Horn*.

I suppose Kirk Douglas is the winner too but somehow
it's easier to type *Lauren Bacall is the winner so far*
with an old fashioned typewriter on a wooden desk
thinking of her.

TIME TIMES

I want to go back to 1952
and eat a lemon chiffon pie
come home and say
Guess what I just did?
to my grandma
who would say
What Dear?
and perish
the next day.

It was her time
and it was
pie time.

LE BON, LA BRUTE, LE TRUAND

The Good, The Bad, and the Handsome.
I think. They are all so good looking.
And isn't it interesting that bad, in French
has a feminine article. I don't think that's right.
It should be neutral. We are neutral.
Here it is simple *the*. But it doesn't make
cowboys less appealing. Or the movie less enticing.
Or less mouth-watering.

Maybe it's just the background on the poster.
It's burnished and yellow.
It almost looks like a chicken pot pie
with cigarillos and beards
instead of carrots and peas.

WIENER DOG

We all laugh when we see dachshunds run.
But we also all go to the dictionary when
we have to spell dachshund. This is something
that makes dachshunds laugh and when they do,
we chase them out of the foyer into the garden
with a broom made of wicker straw,
across the fields and into soft sunlight.

POSTIIVELY SHOCKING, 1964

Pushing the ejector seat button on a car is fun although I bet in 10 years you will simply push your cuff link to start your car.

HATS

I never thought about the men that you find beneath hats
but I better start soon because hats are disappearing just
like the bees are disappearing well not just like the bees
men hats are flying away on windy days and the bees
are being smooshed with magic potions by modern men
who sport no hats atop them no more.

DON

I saw Don's black mustache turn white but since his skin
was skinny you could see the mustache except for in
the black and white photographs where he might as well
have shaved and forgotten all about his stylish invisible face
bottom part but none of us who love him will forget because
that's our job to love Don and to love his parts and we love
this part and all the others too and for as long as they are
there and maybe and always we shall: *Goodbye, Don.*

THE COOKIE ORACLE
for Dashiell

I ordered the pistachio cookies from the chef for my son. They looked like they were made for a king! When I told her that, she blushed, and said she would be happy to deliver the cookies personally to my son herself, because:

1) they were made of pistachio
2) they looked like they were made for a king
3) perhaps someday my son would be king.

THINGS THAT GO WELL WITH YELLOW

There are better ways to communicate your feelings than telegrams but since they still exist (I think) then perhaps there are certain things that are best expressed in telegrams. I wonder what those things are?

BIOGRAPHY OF THE MOON AND A GIRL

She learned how to drive a car on the same night
that the moon came out from behind the old pine trees.

ASSIMILATION

With its blinking lights and massive structures, this room
so filled with obsolete computers could be a city to live in
if you were the size of a marmoset or a thimble
and weren't afraid of so much information
and the more technical aspects of city dwelling.

I WANT TO MARRY A LIGHTHOUSE

Any lighthouse. I'm not too particular.
As long as it has a light that works
and adores me and the funny things
I often say about the sea.

CLIMATE CHANGE

I walk outside to get the newspaper.
And there is no newspaper outside.

Walking inside, I can't help but notice the newspaper.
It is being torn apart by wild coyotes on television.

YOU REALLY WOULD LOVE THE MOON TONIGHT

I went to the Western Union office last night
and asked them to send you this heavengram.

POSSESSED

is a good movie.
You see it and you want to say
"possessed" all the time.

"Come again, " you say to your friend,
"unless you feel possessed."

"This cereal is so delicious,
I fear it might be possessed."

"My second child was named Adam;
my third, Possessed."

"Mmm, nice soda. it's sweet with
just a hint of possessed."

The mark of a good movie is how often
it makes you want to say its title.

Possessed is a good movie.

Although I have forgotten all
the possessed parts.

THE LESSER ESCAPE

I wait until my wife is asleep
and then I hurry down to the kitchen
to have a sip of root beer.

I have done this every night
for the last fifty years.

It used to be so much easier to do.

I was thin and strong
my hair wasn't grey
root beer cost a nickel
and the moon was almost full

MY FAVORITE THING TO SAY
DURING A MYSTERY MOVIE

Yes, He does look like the kind of man who could kill his wife.

X MARKS THE SPOT

Right now I am standing on a staircase.
A hundred years ago I would be standing
on an apple tree. Or perhaps sitting in the
branches of an apple tree. Someday man
will live long enough to sit in an apple tree
that gradually turns into a staircase and
then dies. Of course once the apple tree
staircase dies, the man would have to
die, too, or move to another apple tree
or learn how to construct things that
suspend men in the air as is their want
or their desire or against their will.

THEY SHARED AN UNQUENCHABLE LOVE
Movie posters that are seventy years old

They make me
happy.

They make me curious
about the things
I don't understand

people who
pretended
to be other
people

who often wore
fancy hats
kissed each other
and said
I love you

and then
poof!
magic!

they're
posters

MODERN CONVENIENCES

If you walk a hundred feet back, you can see the sea foam is hand-packed in a tremendous ice cream cone of extraordinary size.

DEVILED HAM DIP

When the house was burning down, she raced into it
to save all her recipes even though she never cared much
for the one her Mother always kept on top.

JIGGLES

I envy people who can draw in straight lines
and wonder how they can do it.

I suspect they feel confident that they can
do it and so they just do it.

I imagine at one time I might have
thought that I could do it.

I wonder if someone had come up
to me and said "Do it!" if I could
have done it.

I think I probably could have unless
as I began I heard someone whisper
"He'll never do it."

I fear then once he did I couldn't and
I would say "I doubt I ever will."

I know if this person wasn't there I could.
I am not going to tell you this person's name.

I will not give him that dignity.

I will call him Sam.
Sam is his real name.
As far as I'm concerned.
He is my evil thing.

Hi Sam.

TREASURE HUNT

The aroma of roasting peppers
outside next to a table covered
with muscadine grapes near
the best house on the street
with the small opened windows
blowing tiny kisses
apple pie kisses
towards us
for no good reason

REQUIEM

I stood in the summer meadow
and solemnly removed my hat
for all the perfect snowmen that
stood here once, bravely
defending their civilization.

GPS REDUX

How does someone so young
know every road in the world?

GEO-ECO POLITICS

If I walk to the left, I am at the gym.
If I walk to the right, I am at the market.

If I walk around the world, I am right here.
If I stay still, something funny will happen.

Like that boulder might move a little.
Towards the gym and the flowerbed.

A goose might suddenly appear.
On the roof. *Voilà*.

It happened once.
I saw it.

I was mowing a lawn.
At my girlfriend's house.

A SECOND ODE TO BUDDY RICH

Sometimes the sound of someone
breaking into a house sounds like
those old Ludwig snare drums
that Buddy Rich used to play.

I love the way that the stick
would sound on the metal rim
of the snare.

I never understood how Buddy Rich
could smoke so many cigarettes
and still play so well.

I used to have a lot of Buddy Rich albums
but most of them have been stolen.

I wonder if Buddy Rich ever stole anything
like an album or a toothbrush.

I wonder why Buddy Rich wore clothes
that just looked so dumb and silly but
they kind of looked cool and swingin'
and 'with it' at the same time.

I wonder if Buddy Rich ever coughed.

Will you look at that puny drum set.

It's tiny.

Buddy's real name was Bernard,

just like Barney Fife's.

I wonder why some people's faces
just look angry,
even when they are asleep.
Or feeling pleasant.

What can you do with genes.

Really there is nothing.

No one could play the drums
like Buddy Rich before he went
to heaven.

And he is everywhere.

I used to even hear Buddy Rich
when I was playing tennis.

And when I was mowing the lawn
or beeping the horn because of
that stupid guy in the Datsun.

Buddy Rich.

What an elegant man,

Kind of.

Laughing with Johnny Carson
smoking, both.

Buddy Rich:

Traps
The Drum Wonder
Buddy Rich.

Bernard Rich.

Mr. Rich.
I miss Buddy Rich.
And I miss Johnny Carson.

More.

Oh, Johnny. Oh John.

Sweet Jackie. Oh John.

This is an ode

To Johnny Carson.

WISHING WELL

You might think you want to be a fish but imagine
swimming without your arms.

Imagine not being able to breathe while you
are staring into the Grand Canyon.

Imagine how little you could do with
a nice Steinway, and the loss of bologna on rye.

Imagine the new pornography.

FOR MY BIRTHDAY

I would like to have a banana split sitting
on the steps of somebody famous
I have never seen in my life, resting atop
a thick warm blanket, blue.

This somebody, if they had a great name,
well, that would be super.

One great name is *Leonard Bernstein*.

Another great name is *Consuelo Butterworth*.

DUSTY

I have a friend who is made of dust and I don't feel sorry
for him because everywhere you go there is dust and so
everywhere he goes he has a friend or would have a friend
if he knew how to mingle with his own but alas he chooses
instead to sit on the couch and dream of the day when he will
meet fresh fruit at the grocer or perhaps a glamorous model
from a magazine, while adorning a magazine.

THAT BEAR

The French and their Cognac were defeated by a girl
named Brandy

with her whiskey and her funny coat which was made
from a bear

but you mustn't cross her as cross her once did
a bear.

THIS IS PROBABLY NOT A POET

I wanted to write a poem today because I wanted
someone special to read it

but she probably won't although she might.
This is no reason to write a poem

or is it the best one. *Hey! Look over there!*
A broken pay phone,

Oh My Love...

WINDOW

I am looking at Jimmy Stewart's chest as he puts on
his blue pajamas. I feel a little bad about that.
But if Alfred Hitchcock didn't want me to look
at Jimmy Stewart's chest, he would have had
Jimmy Stewart say "Excuse me" and go
to the bathroom to change into his blue pajamas.
But there he is in his bedroom holding onto
his blue pajamas.

Jimmy Stewart flew 20 combat missions
with the 703rd Bomb Squadron,
445th Bombardment Group of the Eighth
Air Force during World War II.
Eventually he was promoted to colonel.
He retired when he was an old man,
living in Beverly Hills, growing roses.

I am looking at Jimmy Stewart's chest .
He doesn't look like he has many muscles
beneath his blue pajamas.

Now John Wayne had no pajamas –
and John Wayne
he had no plane
he had muscles. And John Wayne –
well –
he had a big sombrero.

COSTUME

I ate a hamburger on Halloween and by the time I was finished
everyone had dressed up into a costume and everyone had gone crazy.
Not me: I went into a movie house instead and saw a movie about a crazy
person dressed in a white shirt with a crisp collar unbuttoned at the neck.
It wasn't until much later that I discovered that this was a costume. In fact,
what I was wearing to see it was a costume. The movie theatre, also,
was a costume. Those birds outside? A costume. Except for that one,
walking across the street on Halloween, looking straight ahead as the cars
begin to scream and honk.

THE TRUTH ABOUT LOVE

The man who served me pancakes was named Perez.
I did not know that until I went to bed and found
the receipt in my trousers pocket. If only I had known,
I would have said:

*Perez! These pancakes are yummy, even though
I do not, as a rule, fancy pancakes.*

HAZEL

Hazel filled the football with helium and the old lawyer kicked it as hard as he could and it went over one house and stuck in the chimney of another. The old couple in a house had a fire going in their fireplace and the smoke soon filled the room. If Hazel had known, she would have raced into the house to save them, but Hazel isn't real: she is just a character in a television show, and everything she says is written on a piece of paper, and even everything she does is written on a piece of paper, and she has no paper that says: run into the house and save the old couple from certain death, because the old people are also not real people either, even though they are old, and by now, they are gone, for certain, as real people go, for many years have passed since Hazel went over to a man and said, "Do you mind if I fill this football with helium?" and the man, who also wasn't real, replied, "Now why would you want to go and do a thing like that?"

AT STALIN'S FUNERAL

No one was crying
but everyone was frowning

CALAMINT

I am hairy or you might say fuzzy
and about as tall as a small boy.

I am part purple.
And I smell like a tangerine –
an exploding one.

Pregnant women
stay away from me –
they are so smart.

Everyone else says
Hi, Hello there!

My friends call me Monkey.
Or Basil. Or Limestone.

And I live in the sun
like a postage stamp.

What do I do?
What I do is hard to say.

Have you ever used the word
poultice? That is me, in a way.

It's what I do when I walk
into a room and I see

A bruise. Or contusion.
Or some sort of trouble.

I become a poultice.
I get to work.

And I am popular
with animals.

Butterflies and bees
for instance,
find me handsome.

And I, them.

For that I am
thankful.

When I am outside
with my friends

I am happy

And I am even happy

swimming

or not swimming

in a glass of cold tea.

TIME TRAVEL

In my dream, toilet paper was called vanity paper.

ALFRED HITCHCOCK WAS AFRAID OF EGGS

Was it the shape or the color or the sound of breaking one open
on the side of a dish

or the taste or the smoothness or the memory of being born
or the feeling of choking

was it an egg, a whole egg, was in your mouth or the feeling of eggs
when they are cold in

an icebox or was it the way they look on a plate scrambled with
a cigarette smooshed into them

next to a cup of coffee or was it the feeling you have staring at it
for hours and thinking

that can't possibly be the way you spell egg or is it the way a chicken
looks when she

delivers her baby or could it be the feeling you have when you wake up
and you are in

the country and you want to be in the city and next to you is
an egg, an egg, I don't know why,

a regular egg right there, just staring at you

NOVEMBER 7TH

It's the 7th of November again
just like last year and the year before
that and the year before that it was the 6th

of November because I forgot to pull off
the page from the calendar and I lived
a life of confusion for one day and it was
not the best day of my life but it almost
was no

the best day of my life was the day
I ate my first orange

I was approximately
three

the next day Sally got run over by a car.

It wasn't my fault. Still

The next day was the third best day of my life.

Because the playful ghost
of Sally said WOOF!

licked me on my face

and wanted
to play and fetch

DIARY OF A YOUNG BOY

When I buy toy soldiers, I take it very seriously.
After all, they are soldiers.

KISS AND MAKE UP

I wish I could go back in time to
the day when someone told me
how important Harvard was
and I could say: "No it's not!"

and punch them in the face
with a rolled up newspaper
from Spain

it has an article on page two

a tasty recipe
for acorns and wine

THE POEM WAS NEAR PERFECT

Once I changed the word "Spain"
to "Madrid" and then back again
to "Spain."

PETUNIA

I always thought it was "Petulia Clark"
but it was "Petula Clark." Fifty years of
saying "Petulia" makes me feel as though
Petula Clark did something unforgivable
to me. Think of all those people to whom
I once said: "Why don't we go listen to
DOWNTOWN, by Petulia Clark?" How
embarrassing! As though I listened to
petunias. On the other hand, all the kids
thought I was great and thought I was cool
when they heard that great DOWNTOWN
by Petulia Clark and then I snagged them
some frosty cookies and Hawaiian Punch
in Dixie Cups from the third drawer in
the butler's pantry

NO: we didn't have a real butler. But still
I had dreams of butlers. They were always in
teeny bathing suits and smiling and offering things
from the pantry to others who sat near
the record player who were usually in suits
the color of Hawaii and smoking green cigarettes.

CARVING THE MEAT

It's just a little cut on my hand, but if it grew, like bamboo,
I would eventually die. But we are having dinner and I want
to play the piano! So it's settled: *the cut will remain modest.
Love, God.* For this I am grateful to chance, *Lord,* I said. *No —
it's not chance.* You said. *Now where are*

the fire candles?

GALAXIES

If you look at the galaxies in just the right light, they looks like whales and pink peacocks. But if you are old and tired, they looks like pink and black splotches, sort of like a beat-up face, or one of those sexy black-clad photographs from the '60's that you found disturbing and yet, like the galaxies themselves, secretly arousing – so much so, you hid these galaxies from your mommy.

TRUE LOVE ISN'T NICE

When I finally broke down the door, you were standing in the middle of the room and the flames were licking your feet. You looked so pretty there in the dark that I got down on my knees and kissed them: you smiled and called me your secret flame.

THE THEFT OF MONA LISA (1911)

Once there was a Mona Lisa
and then just four crooked nail holes
and a violin, and now there is
a Mona Lisa, covering four
nail holes and there is
no violin

SCHNAPPS

Perhaps the only thing I ever drank because
I liked the way it felt when I said it.

THE BEST PLACE TO WRITE

The best place to write is on a train. Sometimes one word you write can be in Sarasota, and the next word you write can be in Whitfield, and then, Bayshore Gardens. But if the train stops, you will be writing only in Bayshore Gardens. And you throw away all your writing about orange groves, and decide instead to write about trains. The train starts up and you stop. Outside the window are oranges and more oranges. A man with a big cigar.

The train grows hot, it is in flames, orange flames,
you write.

THE MOVIE STAR

I wish fewer people would say I love you.

THE MOVIE STAR

Long ago, it sounded like a movie and a beautiful shimmering star a million miles away in a black sky late at night instead of just a movie person.

THE MOVIE STARS

Speak in an altered *Esperanto*.

WITNESS PROTECTION

In the movie, the boy and the girl sit on the park bench
and look at the sun rise over the ocean. Once the movie
was complete, the boy left for New York, the girl for Idaho,
and the park bench was removed and used for firewood in Maine.

A HISTORY OF NEW YORK

It just occurred to me: the people who built the Empire State Building were extremely brave and virile and wore summer hats as they balanced high in the air and they hooted and whistled and smoked big cigars and now they are dead.

CHAMBERS OF COMERCE

My favorite parking spot at the grocery store is in the third lane from the street
next to the giant oak tree and across from the Spotted Dog restaurant. I like
that spot because it's nice to get out of the car and see that restaurant and think
about all the restaurants and things it's been (The Spotted Dog was once
The Spring Garden, for instance, and years ago, The Tidy Shoe Shoe Store)
and to consider its funny shape, its almost appealing shape (sort of
a triangle, more like a wedge of pie, sliced to order.) The street
where the restaurant lies comes to a point like a pencil tip and
the restaurant is designed the same way. It's really more like
a pie than a wedge, a pie made out of bricks that smells like
soy burgers and leather boots, because of all the burgers
inside and all the people in boots outside. During the day,
everybody is here, but late at night, only the rock 'n rollers
come across the street and drink coffee and eat hash browns
at the restaurant after the bands have stopped playing in the club next door.
The stop lights run all night in front of the restaurant, albeit for no reason after
midnight, and the music ends and it gets very serene. It's nice and a little lonely
to watch the stop lights change colors without a car for miles around, especially
when there is a breeze that comes and goes, swaying the lights.

ONE MAN WAS A GHOST

One man was a ghost.
And another was not.
They were good friends.
Despite their differences.

How they loved to eat
hamburgers together.
And talk about nothing.

PIZZA

I would like to die ordering a pizza
listening to the voice of a woman
I always wanted to meet

I only called her because PIZZA
is right next to person I wish
I knew on my contact list

I would love to read that the person
I wish I knew worked at the pizza house
that I loved to order pizza from only

I didn't know It so actually
I dialed the right number after all
my fingers were working perfectly

Right until the end – as worked the courage
of my heart – I would love to read about
it all in the newspaper well, I would like

Somebody to read about it and tell me
how it all worked out someday
when maybe we get together again
in a place where we can still enjoy
eating pizza or the thought of doing
so together.

INSIDE THE KAZOO FACTORY

Because I want to learn to make an instrument
that try as you may, cannot be played
mournfully

HOLLYWOOD CANTEEN

In the movie, they go to the back of the house
where it is dark so they can make out
until her parents come home and he must
sneak out through the little white gate
and get on the train
and go back to the war
but first – a kiss

BALD

There is nothing that you can talk about when you talk about baldness because you would be talking about something that isn't anything.

A KISS ON SATURDAY IN JULY

I wish we knew
when we were
doing something
for the last time.

BAKING COOKIES PT 4

Roll the cookie dough in a 1 1/2 diameter log and wrap it in wax paper and tuck into the refrigerator for approximately two hours. Once firm, retrieve the sleeping cookie dough from the fridge and roll into the East River at dawn. Make sure that no one is following you and if they are oh boy you are in trouble with Mr. Cookie now.

Run as fast as you can, buster! / if you are not a smoker!

INSTEAD

I have never known a woman with a name that began with Z.
I have never known a woman who had a Z in her name.
When I went to England, they told me that Z is Zed,
and that William Blake is dead,
and that the most beautiful color is red,
although sometimes it is orange,
orange like a peach.

LONGSTREET

There was a wonderful show on television in 1971
and it was all about the adventures of a blind detective
or so I thought. The blind detective was actually a blind
insurance investigator with a boss who had a lush mustache
and wide lapels and curly hair and looked like a porn star
which was a great way to look in 1971 on television everyone
loved that look for some reason and now we love it too for
some reason but we don't know the reason back then nor do
we know the reason right now but still we love it well – really,
these days, let's admit it, we love it, and just about everything.

IN THE NEWS

Many bananas were upset that they fell out of a truck.
But they were happy that it was a foggy day.
Bananas love foggy days.
Bananas love trucks.
Not falling.
Or roads.
Scientists are uncertain as to why.
Scientists understand so many things
But Scientists don't always understand
what lies deep
within the heart
of the everyday banana.

WHY I LIKE SILK

Because silk is silk, not silky

LIGHT

Sometimes I think, if the lightbulb goes out in your lamp,
it's better to just throw the lamp away. Every time you buy
a new lamp, the light in your room will be a little different
and once again you will own a whole new room.

DRESSING IN LAYERS

If you place one photo of a man's face over one photo
of a woman's face, and you do it again and again and again,
eventually, it will become a woman's face.

DIVINE

I once knew a man who could twist a balloon into funny shapes. On some days I was a very special balloon who escaped his reach and could run away and remain plain.

LETTER OF REFERENCE

Inside of this medium egg is a tremendously large yolk.

LIFE STORY

Three dots and a question mark

PING PONG

An old photograph of Paris.
A city I don't know.

There is a little shop, a
boulangerie, that might
offering cheap sweets.

The air above the streets
looks almost purple.

The sign for *boulangerie*
is an orange horseshoe

a donut with one bite
taken. It reminds me

of a bakery in Texas
as you drive by slowly

in a small car
at sunset while

smoking le petite
cigar

driving
towards Idaho

FOUND POEM NAMED KYBELLA

can cause nerve damage
and uneven smile

1967

I loved getting up Saturdays at dawn
and riding my bicycle in the dark
to the 7-11 and buying a Cherry Slurpee
there while waiting for Sandy to put out
the new comic books in the rack while
sitting on the floor and eating my
Cracker Jacks and Mallow Cup
and dreaming about how much
fun it would be to own
a motorcycle. A red
motorcycle. A red
motorcycle and a
mustache like
the kind next
to the comic
books in the
motorcycle
magazines
at dawn
near the
hardworking
morning hands
of Sandy *

* see notes

ADIEU

I plunge my fork into a pea
and lift the pea unto the light
and see the steam rise off the pea
and then then I say goodnight, pea
goodnight

CHIMNEY SWEEPS

I hate bicycles on album covers
and on cigarette labels and
underneath portly firemen
who say Hallo! and I hate
bicycles made out of candy
and bicycles made out of
quinoa, too, when it is too fussy
and when Mao rides a bicycle I hate
Mao & his bicycle and when I am singing
My Cherie Amor I hate the bicycle that
is on a Christmas tree somewhere in
a house although I don't know where
although I love Christmas when I come
down before the sun is up and right there
in the living room next to the stereo console
and a ashtray filled with Viceroys is a brand new
bicycle and perhaps it is mine, next to it is a glass
of whiskey and a dame and a good book and a glass
of fresh-squeezed orange juice and another bicycle.
A beautiful bicycle. Maybe that one's mine not
the other one.

Let's just face it: I hate some kinds of bicycles and not others.

ANYONE

Writing a love letter and putting it in the mailbox sealed in an envelope addressed to Anyone / USA and writing it in disappearing ink

is something I do that every day, Sally said.

TRUE LOVE

Alice told me a story about a man she dated
whom she christened Mr. Tool Belt and I asked
why and the answer was both peculiar and unusual.

FORD COUNTRY SQUIRE, 1960:
Queen of the Station Wagon Kingdom

The color of upholstery ("ribbed Morocco bolstering
and pleated inserts") was often like chocolate and
the shape of the ridges were similarly chocolate bar-like.
Panels ran along the sides of the station wagon that
were either made of wood

or of a wood facsimile ("di-hoc mahogany appliqué
with 'maple' fiberglass trim.") Like chocolate, or
the impression of chocolate, or pancakes, or
the appearance of pancakes, it gave comfort.

On the driver's side left, an antennae was often extended
fully and suggested that we were in touch with worlds that
we couldn't possibly comprehend or reach; it made a faint
buzzing sound in the wind. This too, was a pleasant sensation,
rather than a fearful one.

Yet between the mother and the father, tucked away
center deep, was a cigarette lighter which reminded us
that this could all go away someday, and do so in a burst
of light, but not if we managed to keep everything as it was
and where it was meant to be, and enjoyed the things that
seemed like chocolate and wood, and warmth, the sensation
of those things, those things which seemed to be our slight gifts.

CITY LIFE

Beautiful car horns,
I miss you when
you're not there

COUNTRY LIFE

Beautiful car horn,
I miss you when
you're not there

INSOMNIA

As you write a note at the kitchen table
and you hear the sound of a leaf
falling to the earth

Don't blame yourself
there's nothing you
could have done

NINETEEN THIRTY-FIVE MOVIES

To sell a newspaper
You must wear a cap.
You must be little.
And you must scream.

SILENT MOVIE

Sound is just a nuisance. Especially in movies.
Last night I was watching a Clint Eastwood
movie so very quietly and Clint Eastwood
was ordering a cup of coffee. The waitress
put a lot, I mean a whole lot of sugar in his
coffee and he wasn't paying attention because
he was reading the paper. As he walked out
he tasted it and went PAH-FHEW! and spit
it out and came back to complain and lo!
there were a bunch of hoodlums holding guns,
all pointed smack dab at the waitress.

Clint looked at them and said something
about the weather, so brisk and clear in
the Archipelago, and the bad hoodlums
said something about never having visited
the Archipelago, although they certainly
wouldn't mind a brief holiday, what,
with the weather being like it is and all,
and Clint looked really angry and said
that he seldom ate blueberry cheesecake,
especially on days like today, Arbor Day,
which he scarcely remembered unless
his wife reminded him of the holiday,
his wife gone now, lo these many years —
isn't it funny that he happened to remember this time?

For some reason this really made the bandidos angry,
and yet when I turned up the sound, all I could hear
was firecrackers on the Fourth of July, and what
sounded like an old Cab Calloway record being run
over by a truck going backwards in a jiffy, and which
really seemed to interrupt the flow of conversation
so I just turned it off. As Clint left the bar, he said —

I am certain – something about the how merry
the month of June was, which I could understand,
even though it is hot, why, even mountains, along
the balmy coast, how they almost seem to weep
from the sheer joy of being alive and themselves
on such a day as this, such a beautiful day as this...

SILENT INVENTORY

When Oliver Hardy kicked a football, it went down five flights of stairs and hit a man right in the head and his hair fell forward and he looked just like one of the Beatles! Although his hair was somewhat sandy, which reminded me more of the Beach Boys' Dennis Wilson, and he was angry, because of the football, which reminds me of my great grandmother, Ignatia, who detested football in all its forms, mostly because, she hated everything, and everything in all its forms, which makes me laugh now. Oh thank you Granmummy, for making me laugh this rainy day in December! Although it isn't raining yet. It probably really won't. But sometimes you just get this feeling in your bones. I remember the Beach Boys said this in one of their songs. I forget who sang it –
I think it was the dead one.

THE BERMUDA TRIANGLE

If you wear a three cornered hat, you are eccentric.
But if you wear a three cornered hat indoors,
your head remains warm in the summer, and warm
in the winter, and you are eccentric.

OWNER'S REMORSE

I wasn't certain why I had bought a black rotating fan
instead of the pink one, which was a much prettier fan.
But one night when the moon came out, I could see the moon,
just a sliver, glowing white, reflected in the black metal of the fan.

Until it rotated away from me. When it rotated back, I could see
it again. I could see the moon. The moon was in my fan. Again
and again, I saw the moon, then didn't, in my black fan.

I stayed up almost all night that night. When the sun began
to rise, the sky was pink.

THE STORY OF A LIKABLE CHAP

Andrew Jackson shot to kill. But he didn't always shoot to kill.
At first he used to shoot up in the air. Then he shot to maim.
Sometimes in the groin region. Perhaps he thought it was funny.
Although it was terrifying, for not only men of that century,
but also for birds. Of all the Presidents, Andrew Jackson
was the most feared by all birds. Until Teddy Roosevelt.
But even the birds agreed that there was something likable
about Teddy Roosevelt. But that didn't stop them from dying
when he took out his Holland & Holland Double. And die they did.
Oh yes indeedy. That likable chap, he shot them aplenty.

He didn't mean any harm. He just wanted to shoot them.

MAY I HELP YOU

I bought an oxford cloth shirt that I thought was white.
It was green.
But a light green, like a Crayola.
I couldn't stop smelling its beautiful green.
It reminded me of an old lady's perfume.
A nice old lady.
In a Spring snow.
Once she fell down in that snow.

ZELDA & THE THISTLES

I should have been paying attention to my 18th century book
the one that described the weather as 'chill' and the one
where the father played with his his little boy and thistles
by the lake

But I couldn't stop thinking about the presents I should give
for Christmas this year – at first I thought of lavender cookies
and then I thought no, most people love chocolate best of all

And then I thought Why not give a book of paintings made
by someone who paints really well

And no one knew could paint at all? Her mother tried to burn them all,
they scared her, I am not sure why, they were beautiful

With that it was easy then to return to the lake, and
the little boy with thistles

Be careful! Thistles!

and making a tiny ship of paper
and walking to the old post office through the woods
and feeling a little lonely
when suddenly someone says hello, or ¡Hola!
in Spanish, someone with a big ol' *sombrero*, why –
It's Herman Melville! Seriously! Herman Melville!

Hi, Herman!

PAT & HIS EX-LOVER, EX-PAT

This white wine I found, that I want to share with you,
from Portugal, is called Home of the Wolf, or Little Home
of the Wolf, or Hut of the Wolf, I think. I don't want to look
it up in the dictionary, because it might mean The Little Wolf,
or Look, a Wolf!, or A Small Woof, which is what you hear
at the door when you have a small dog or wolf who loves
to play outside in Portugal with his squeezee toy until it is so
moist with his mouth juices that you don't want to pick it up.
It's gross, but you love him so much in Portugal and he loves
to play with you so much in Portugal that you pick it up
anyway and throw it as far as it will go. He barks jauntily
as droplets abound and cascade, gracing the countryside
in a profuse glory, until it lands in a field of grass, next door —
still in Portugal.

IT'S 7:00 AND ROAST APPLES

I am missing a nice bulldog and a fireplace
and a nice bulldog looking into my fireplace
I didn't think about this until I looked at the NYer
this week (It's really "The New Yorker" but these lines
are so short that I had to break them up more than wanted)
anyway there was a nice bulldog and a fireplace on its cover
You can tell it's a nice bulldog even though you can only see
it from behind. Dogs and humans are easy to know from
behind. Just look at Eric Roberts from behind for instance.
Or a Mongolian Wolf Hound. But, you might say, there are
some people who don't even have a subscription to the
New Yorker, so I should think of that when I am sad about
my lack of bulldog fireplace.

It's true. Although my subscription was a gift. I love gifts. I am
also thankful for that. I love people who give gifts to me as gifts.
I love giving gifts to people who love them, these gifts.

Yay, Xmas. This year for Xmas, I would like to get the following gifts:
a pair of oven mitts, a trumpet, a penny whistle, a candy bar, and
a new car. This year for Xmas, I would like to give the following gifts:
purple ink for a fountain pen, Ray Bans, French Oreo cookies,
some savory lime caper sauce, Emily Post, and books about how
to survive and be happy in the 19th century.

Of that book, I have multiple copies. I like to give them out,
like peppermints. This year I will give out more than ever.
I must. And after Xmas, I will roast more apples and talk
more often to the sun. I will call the people I love. I can't wait.
It is a new dawn upon the whathaveyou of fireplaced bulldogs.

EN GUARDE

You throw a bottle in the air
and when it starts to come down
you slice it with your saber really fast
right along the neck where it is weakest
all the foamy liquid stops the broken glass
from going back into the bottle

So you can stop your horse
dismount him and say
Good Boy, Gus!
(a peculiar choice for a name)
and after everything is done
you and he

have a tasty sip of
sweet champagne

BIG PILES OF CORN

are something I would like to see someday
but the only way you can see big piles of corn
on a farm is if you see big piles of ears of corn
If that is OK with you but still that just isn't
the same as big piles of corn

in an oak barrel hot and steamy
with little sprigs of thyme, sprinkled

They are small those sprigs of thyme
but there are ten million of them

like little aliens from
an old tv show
looking for love
in Iowa

DOLL

A couple bought a doll for their little girl who refused to play with it. They stored it in the attic for many years, and one day, when they came upon it, it had aged terribly, and appeared to be an old woman; gaunt, and close to death.

"Well, that's depressing," the wife said to her husband.
And it was.

CANDY BAR

Once a little girl asked her father if she could buy a gigantic candy bar
from the store. Her father loved her dearly and could not refuse her.
"Yes," he said, and she did. Three years later when she went to the dentist,
and had a terrible cavity. The dentist took pity upon the little girl and gave her
a small ring to wear on her finger - one with a beautiful plastic ruby setting.

The little girl wore the ring until the day she died, about a week later, when
she was hit by a truck that was carrying spring onions to the marketplace
on Chestnut Street.

THE YOUNG MAN

The young man ordered the venison dish with chestnuts because he had never eaten a chestnut and lately had wondered if they even existed. When the waiter brought out the venison, he apologized that there were no chestnuts. The young man was then certain that surely, chestnuts must exist, for as the waiter apologized, he wept.

A LITTLE BOY

Once a little boy went to the circus to see the elephants.
The elephants looked sad and that made the little boy sad.
The little boy asked his father for a quarter to buy a floaty
balloon for the elephant to cheer him up, even though the
balloon was only 15¢. His father gave him a quarter and
the boy hurriedly raced over to the elephant with his
new red balloon. The elephant stared at the little boy.
The little boy chewed a stick of bubble gum and jingled
his pocket change.

The balloon.

LITTLE CIRCLES, TRIANGLES, DOTS

The little boy swam in circles for hours.
And then he swam in little triangles.
And then in little dots. His father came out to
fetch him, swimming in a straight line. He returned to shore
by way of a wobbly line. The line looked like a cane that
someone left out in the sun under a tree.

NOGGIN

You know when you say 'you should always use your noggin' and then you tap on your noggin that you are actually tapping on a bone-colored skull that makes you scream in monster movies and can do absolutely nothing for itself other than be happy that even by doing nothing people are screaming and running away from you the skull even though their skulls are the things that are doing all the screaming.

STRATEGY

I enjoy a small town, a little town, a town that you can put in your pocket, a town that is fragrant but still wholesome, a town that is chewy but still digestible, a town with a name that has nothing to do with size, or shape, or meaning – a town you forget once you have eaten it and moved on to a city, and then back, again, to a town.

LOST LOVE

The recipe called for cranberries that are stripped of their clothes and put into a bowl and then boiled alive for the pleasure of dessert.

HIGH SCHOOL REUNION

Let's admit it: we all look terrible,
and the handsome ones by now
are dead, at least
to us.

GROCERY LIST

Baby Peas
Sweet Little Baby Peas
Sweet and Frozen Little Baby Peas
A big bag of Baby Peas
Sweet and Frozen and Little

Oh peas

Dear, dear
peas

You feel so nice
in my mouth
and on
my skull

MY FAVORITE PICTURE OF WILLIAM CARLOS WILLIAMS

He is posed in a Model T with a small boy who could only be his son and he looks exotic and Middle Eastern with an air of mystery and perhaps adventure. As he grew older, he just looked like an old man who couldn't find his car in the parking lot at Target.

We all do that sometimes — lose our Target cars. But we never appear mysterious when we do; we look poetic, once he gets out of his car, walks inside, sits at that little wooden table, and pulls out a small pencil from his pocket.

EVERY VOICE IS FAMOUS TO SOMEONE

Every Voice is Famous to Someone

THE THERAPY OF BLISS

They sat together on the couch and held hands
for twenty minutes.

They released their hands when the egg timer's bell rang.

HEARTBREAK

I used to own a wonderful set of drums and I recently replaced it with a metronome from Sweden where the national flower is the *Linnea Borealis*, or "Twinflower" – a flower that is pink, bell-like and fragrant, and grows in pairs.

acknowledgments

*a big thank you to the periodicals that published
the following works, some in slightly altered forms:*
(in order of appearance)

Ice Drumming (Otolith)
Snow Globe (Setu Magazine)
Poughkeepsie (Queen Mob's Teahouse)
The Different Parts of the Orchestra (Spinoza Blue)
What Happens When You Die (Blue Mountain Review)
1961 (The Sacred Cow)
Secret Service (Blue Mountain Review)
Behest (Spinoza Blue)
A Slinky Has No Choice (Bitchin' Kitsch)
Wishing Well (Birds Piled Loosely)
Deep Freeze (Birmingham Art Journal)
Cartoon (Lunaris)
Conduct (Chiron Review)
Carrot (Chiron Review)
Rapscallions (Bitchin' Kitsch)
Playing the Piano in a Sporting House (Oddball Magazine)
Still, It's Nice To Be Kissed (Picaroon Poetry)
My First Wife (Open Mouse)
Tomorrow Never Knows (Yes, Poetry)
Science TV (Setu Magazine)
Sumerian Proverbs (Setu Magazine)
Fresh Donuts of Laundry in Space (Otolith)
Since We All Die (Moonglasses)
Purple Car (Ink, Sweat & Tears)
Someone Stole Anna Pavlova's Slippers (Backslash)
Action (Red Fez)
Dear John (Literary Yard)
Hat (Literary Yard)
Don (Literary Yard)
Le Bon, La Brute, Le Truand (Full of Crow)
I Want To Marry a Lighthouse (Literary Yard)
Costume (Bitchin' Kitsch)
Hazel (Unbroken Journal)
Calamint (Apricity Press)
Words That Rhyme (Apricity Press)
Pentunia (Apricity Press)
A History of New York (Praxis Magazine)
Divine (Birds Piled Loosely)
Insomnia (Eunoia Magazine)
Therapy of Bliss (Eunoia Magazine)

• notes •

Dear Reader,

I apologize. In the poem referenced I mention a morning at dawn at the convenience store, and how on that morning I enjoyed eating a Mallow Cup. The truth is, I have never eaten a Mallow Cup. They are made with Marshmallows. I hate marshmallows. What I ate was a cup all right, but it was a Reese's Peanut Butter Cup. Why I said I had eaten a Mallow Cup instead, I don't know; perhaps it was that Reese's Peanut Butter Cups has too many words in it and also sounds a bit like a kind of monkey. I wanted to convey the feeling of joy at dawn at the convenience store, that special joy, with not too many words and definitely *sans* monkeys.

I also wanted to convey the feeling of eating chocolate at dawn. The sheer pleasure of it. And sitting outside a convenience store, all dark outside, waiting for it to open, and that feeling of bliss. They have the best comic books in convenience stores. And super great candy and Cherry Icees. The man at the counter, Sandy, is really great. He always waves to me while I sit outside. It's a warm tropical morning. It's warm outside and inside it is cool.

I wrote this because I am pretty certain that this morning dawn outside the convenience store was the best day of my life. I guess that's kind of sad. That was the best day of your life? But it's not sad. No, actually, it's really happy. It was a great day. It's the day I love most. Ask some people about the happiest day of their lives and they pause and think for a while and say "I just don't know", sadly shake their heads and begin to weep. It's awful. I feel terrible for them. I hate that they must weep. I hate that anyone weeps. I just wish I could hold all these people in my arms until we all stopped.

Love,

The Author

www.ingramcontent.com/pod-product-compliance
Lightning Source LLC
Chambersburg PA
CBHW020731160426
43192CB00006B/189